John Blacket

A South Australian Romance

How a Colony was Founded and a Methodist Church Formed

John Blacket

A South Australian Romance
How a Colony was Founded and a Methodist Church Formed

ISBN/EAN: 9783337008024

Printed in Europe, USA, Canada, Australia, Japan

Cover: Foto ©ninafisch / pixelio.de

More available books at **www.hansebooks.com**

A

SOUTH AUSTRALIAN ROMANCE

HOW A COLONY WAS FOUNDED

AND A

METHODIST CHURCH FORMED

BY THE

REV. JOHN BLACKET

SOUTH AUSTRALIA

*"Now shall it be said of Jacob and of Israel,
What hath God wrought?"* Num. xxiii. 23.

London:
CHARLES H. KELLY
2, CASTLE ST., CITY RD.; AND 26, PATERNOSTER ROW, E.C.
1899

"Fellow-Colonists! if this is a proud day to us, as most assuredly it ought to be, how much more should our Brethren, in the dear Old Mother Country, exult in the pride of our situation! How should they rejoice at being witnesses of what no other nation in the world besides England has been permitted to see! What other nation has seen her children so extensively spread over the most distant parts of the earth, founding communities, governing themselves, speaking the same language, improving on the models of her institutions, reverencing the land of their forefathers, and sympathising with that race of which we ourselves are a continuing branch?"—Sir HENRY AYERS, "Address at Jubilee of South Australia, 1886."

TO

THE MEMORY

OF

MY WIFE'S PARENTS

CALEB AND PHŒBE FIDLER

PIONEERS

IN THE ESTABLISHMENT OF METHODISM IN THE

SOUTH-EASTERN PART OF SOUTH AUSTRALIA

THIS BOOK

IS DEDICATED

CONTENTS

CHAP.		PAGE
	AN ACKNOWLEDGMENT	xi
I.	INTRODUCTORY	1
II.	DRAWING THE PLANS	9
III.	PREPARING TO BUILD	23
IV.	LAYING THE FOUNDATIONS	33
V.	RAISING THE SUPERSTRUCTURE	49
VI.	THREE BUILDERS OF METHODIST FAME	73
VII.	HOW A METHODIST CHURCH WAS FORMED	97
VIII.	THE TRAVELLING PREACHER AND HOW HE CAME	121
IX.	HOW THE CHURCH GREW	143
X.	AN ABLE ADMINISTRATOR	171
XI.	AFTER SIXTY YEARS	201

LIST OF ILLUSTRATIONS

	PAGE
SOUTH AUSTRALIAN NATIVE	*Frontispiece*
A SOUTH AUSTRALIAN SCENE	8
PORTRAIT: JOHN CHARLES WHITE	22
PROCLAMATION TREE, HOLDFAST BAY, 1898	32
FIRST WESLEYAN PLAN FOR ADELAIDE CIRCUIT	47
ADELAIDE: HINDLEY STREET, 1846	48
GOVERNMENT HOUSE, ADELAIDE, 1846	70
PORTRAIT: REV. JOHN STEPHENS	72
PORTRAIT: PASTOR JACOB ABBOTT	96
PORTRAIT: REV. WILLIAM LONGBOTTOM	120
CLARENDON	142
PORTRAIT: REV. JOHN EGGLESTON	161
PORTRAIT: REV. DANIEL J. DRAPER	170
ADELAIDE IN 1896: KING WILLIAM STREET	200

AN ACKNOWLEDGMENT

AFTER the lapse of more than sixty years, to " trace the course of all things accurately from the first," is by no means easy. Unless the course is *accurately* traced, the attempt had better not be made. It was in the spirit of this conviction that the writer undertook the present work.

It is not a relation of personal experience. The Colony of South Australia had been founded many years before the writer came out of the mysterious somewhere upon this busy Australian scene. Whilst this is true, the reader will please bear in mind that painstaking effort has been put forth to make the record correct.

It is hardly necessary to add that this has consumed a large amount of time, and has involved a considerable degree of labour. Old records had to be found, and then carefully searched. Like Papias, when seeking apostolic traditions, the writer "imagined that what was to be got from books was not so profitable for him as what came from the living voice," consequently old colonists had to be sought out, and interrogated.

To all who so generously rendered assistance my hearty thanks are due, and are herewith tendered.

JOHN BLACKET.

WESLEYAN PARSONAGE,
MELROSE, SOUTH AUSTRALIA,
July 1898.

A SOUTH AUSTRALIAN ROMANCE

CHAPTER I

INTRODUCTORY

HISTORY is full of romance. There is a peculiar fascination about it. It brings sunshine into our lives, and seems to lengthen out the thread of our existence. As we read the record of what our fathers did in the old time before us the "heart is strangely warmed," and the imagination fired. The mind goes back to a time long anterior to the birth of the body, and the remote past is brought within the range of our experience. We see the battles that our fathers fought. We hear the song of praise and shout of victory. We see them grappling with difficulties, surmounting obstacles, till they have made the rough places smooth, the crooked places straight, and have burst asunder the bars of iron.

Many events in the history of a nation remind us that "fact is stranger than fiction." It is so in the history of the Church. Take the Methodist Church, of which, in the course of the following pages, we shall have to speak. Its history is a modern Acts of the Apostles. It is a marvellous record of the wonder-working power of God. Again we see how God chooses "the weak things of the world to put to shame things that are strong, and things that are not, to bring to nought the things that are."

Surely the *Arminian Magazine* had its genesis in a Divine idea. To John Wesley, in London, as to St. John the Apostle, in Patmos, there came the command: "What thou seest, write in a book." The pages of that book are before us. We are grateful to God for the record they contain. Often has the soul expanded, the spiritual vision become clearer, and the intangible more real when studying the record made by our Methodist Fathers of what God has wrought. Here we see souls transfigured and lives transformed. Here is the record of men and women, in humble spheres of life, who exerted a powerful influence for good. Here we see great issues growing out of small beginnings. "Five chase a hundred, and a hundred chase ten thousand." Here we see the mysterious operations of Providence more fascinating (at least to the Christian) than any fictitious romance. "The appearance of the wheels and their work, was like unto the colour of a beryl; . . . and their appearance and their work was as it were a wheel within a wheel." In our Methodist "Acts of the Apostles" is the experience of men and women who could say: "We are ambassadors, therefore, on behalf of Christ, as though God were entreating by us, we beseech you, on behalf of Christ, be ye reconciled to God. . . . In everything commending ourselves, as ministers of God, in much patience, in afflictions, in necessities, in distresses, in stripes, in imprisonments, in tumults, in labours, in watchings, in fastings. . . . As deceivers, yet true; as unknown, and yet well known; as dying, and behold we live; as chastened, and not killed; as sorrowful, yet always rejoicing; as poor, yet making many rich; as having nothing, yet possessing all things." As the result of this apostolic spirit, and devoted labour, multitudes became "obedient unto the faith."

The canonical "Acts of the Apostles" came to an abrupt close, not so the Methodist record. The work begun by Wesley is still going on, and so is the record of that work.

We said, at the outset, that "fact is stranger than fiction"; we now give a different rendering: "fact is often more fascinating than fiction." Methodism is full of romance—full of stirring incident, strange surprises, and remarkable events. That such is the case we believe some of our pages will show.

The foundation of this Colony, and the formation of the Methodist Church therein, run parallel. They are strangely interlinked. Both will come under review. It is our intention to give—not an up-to-date history of the Colony, nor of the Church, but a vivid picture of early colonial life, and of the romantic circumstances under which a Church was formed, and the pleasing rate at which it grew.

It is not of the whole of Australia that we have to speak; but of *South Australia*. A caution here is necessary. We are so far away from the Old World, and our history, comparatively speaking, is so recent, that our kindred in the Old Land are apt to fall into error. Australia is a vast island-continent, divided into Colonies. Each Colony has an independent existence; it administers its own affairs, and has a Governor appointed by the Crown. It is of the early history of one of these Colonies that we have to speak. A good map of Australia will add much to the instruction and enjoyment of the reader as we show—

"How a Colony was Founded, and a Methodist Church was Formed."

A SOUTH AUSTRALIAN SCENE.

CHAPTER II

DRAWING THE PLANS

THE first known discovery of any part of South Australia was made in 1672. The discoverer was a Dutch navigator. He sailed along the south coast. The new land was called Nuyt's Land. It was so called after a person on board named Peter Nuyt. The honour of a practical discovery of the country belongs to Captain Flinders. In 1802 he surveyed the southern coast, and named its several points. Flinders' Range, at the foot of which these lines were penned, was named after the illustrious navigator.

The first white man to get a glimpse into the interior of South Australia was Captain Sturt. In 1829 the Government of New South Wales commissioned him to trace the course of the Murrum-

bidgee. A whale-boat was secured, and the
necessary provision made. At the head of a party,
Captain Sturt set sail. The trip must have been
a most fascinating one. They were gliding down
a stream on which no white man's boat had ever
been launched; they were passing through country
that no white man had ever seen. The journey
had its difficulties and dangers. Here and there
in the stream were "snags,"—submerged logs,—
against which the boat might strike; there were
rapids to be passed over, with the possibility of
being upset. These added romance to the trip.

After sailing some time down the Murrumbidgee
the boat suddenly shot into a noble river, flowing
from east to west. This proved to be what is now
known as the *Murray*. It was so named by
Captain Sturt in honour of Sir George Murray,
Secretary of State for the Colonies. This must
have indeed been a surprise. The excitement of
the party must have been intense. On the adven-
turers glided, not knowing whither they went,
wondering, no doubt, what other revelations were
in store. Borne on the bosom of the noble river
they sailed past giant gums. Away in the distance

the kangaroo bounded. Occasionally they got a glimpse of some of the natives of the soil. At times they were very hostile. Covered with war paint, brandishing their spears, and sounding their battle-cry, they rushed down to the water's edge. After sailing about two months down the Murray they came to a vast fresh-water lake. This was the reservoir into which the river flowed. This body of water Captain Sturt called Lake Alexandrina, in honour of the Princess who now, as Queen, sits upon the throne. The explorers were now in one of the most romantic parts of South Australia. This was the happy hunting-ground of the blackfellow. On the banks of the Murray, and round the shores of the lake, he built his wurlies, held his corroberies, chanted to his piccaninnies, taught them how to swim, to throw the spear, and to track emus, kangaroos, and enemies. Here he caught his fish, and noosed and netted wild fowl. No wonder that he was both awed and angry when he saw his territory invaded by mysterious whites. The Rev. George Taplin, who spent many years amongst the blacks, in the early days, says: "I know several men who remembered the arrival of Captain Sturt, and they tell of the terror which was felt as they beheld his boat crossing Lake Alexandrina."

Passing over the lake, Captain Sturt discovered the junction of the Murray with the sea.

It was the discoveries made on the coast by Captain Flinders, and in the interior by Captain Sturt, that lay at the basis of the schemes for South Australian colonisation.

As all roads led to Rome, so the history of the Anglo-Saxon race everywhere leads to a national centre. For the colonisation scheme of this vast territory we must turn to England. We have to go back to the time when the " Iron Duke " was taking an active part in politics, and when the great men of Methodism—Bunting, Newton, and Watson— were at their zenith.

In 1829 a "National Colonisation Committee" was formed in London. Its object was to "explain to the public the plan of colonisation on which the new province of South Australia was to be founded." This came to nought. In 1831 a second committee was formed. This also had to be disbanded.

An old print that lies before the writer, published by Ridgway & Sons, Piccadilly, in 1834, gives "the outline of the plan of a proposed Colony to be founded on the south coast of Australia, with an account of the soil, climate, rivers," etc. It gives the prospectus of an Association, the object of which "is to found a Colony under Royal Charter, at or near Spencer's Gulf, on the south coast of Australia." The public is informed that "a Committee sits daily at the office of the Association, 8 Adelphi Chambers, for the purpose of giving information to persons disposed to settle in the Colony."

The "whole of the purchase-money of public land," in the new Colony, "after defraying the necessary cost of survey and sales," was to be "employed in conveying British labourers to the Colony." Emigrants conveyed to the Colony were to be "young people, of the two sexes, in equal number." Preference was to be given to "young married couples without children."

Among other reasons why this part of the world should be colonised by English people, the following are stated :—"There is every reason to believe that the whole of extra-tropical Australia is free from endemic disease. The seaboard advantages of South Australia were great. The magnificent harbour of Port Lincoln would be the chief emporium for the trade of that region, and Coffin's Bay would eventually receive all the produce of the line of the coast to the west. It was expected that the country would yield coal, woods of various kinds, and bark for tanning. Salt fish would find a ready market in Peru, Chili, and the Isle of France. Wheat and flour would find a market in the Isle of France, the Cape, Rio Janeiro, and probably China. Tobacco, flax, hemp, and cotton were to be grown."

In the light of more than sixty years' experience it is refreshing to read the glowing anticipations of those who drew up the colonisation plan. The "magnificent harbour of Port Lincoln" is so far of little use. It was to be the "chief emporium of trade for that region." Unfortunately, all the trade transacted there can be done with a few small boats. Coffin's Bay, which was "to receive all the produce of the west," remains much as it was sixty years ago. The "export of salt fish to Peru, Chili, and the Isle of France," will be one of the surprises of the future. We have done something in the direction of exporting wheat and flour, but the "cultivation of tobacco, flax, hemp, cotton," are parts of the original plan that generations to come must fulfil.

We leave No. 9 Adelphi Chambers and go to Exeter Hall. It is June the 30th, 1834. A great number of people are making their way to the historic building. Carriages are driving up and dropping their occupants. In the manner and address of the people there is great animation. It is a meeting of the promoters and friends of the projected Colony in South Australia. About two thousand five hundred persons, including many Members of Parliament, are present. There is excitement inside as well as out. A man who has caught the radical spirit of the times desires to speak. He rises. "I wish to ask a question." There are cries of "No! No!" and great uproar. "What is the gentleman's name?" the chairman asks. The reply is: "I am Thomas Goode, of Kettering, Northamptonshire, and I repeat that I have a question to ask." (Renewed uproar.) "I am in the hands of the meeting," the chairman says; "it is for you to determine what would be the more convenient course." Thomas Goode sits down. Robert Owen is present, and no doubt feeling an interest in his radical friend, steps into the breach. "I beg to ask," he says, "whether this is to be considered a public meeting, or a meeting of the friends of the system?" "Most unquestionably," the chairman replies, "this is a public meeting; and I may add that it is the object of all who are interested in the undertaking to make the proceedings partake as much of a public character as possible; but in order that a fair opinion may be formed, will it not be better for the subject to be fully before the meeting prior to any gentleman entering into a discussion of its merits?" The chairman has evidently voiced the opinion of the meeting. There are cries of "Hear! hear!" and applause. Several addresses in favour of colonisation are delivered. The meeting is now thrown open. The stranger, who describes himself as "Thomas Goode, of Kettering," again rises, and walks to the front. There are cries of "Off! Off!" and much uproar. "I am one of the productive classes," he says, "who work early in the morning and late at night for the rich." Cries of "Question! Question!" "I congratulate the gentlemen who have formed themselves into a Committee for the purpose of advancing this Association, on their success. I would say to them in the language of Scripture: 'Be not weary in well-doing, for in due time ye shall reap if ye faint not.' . . . Colonel Torrens has said that the gentlemen who sought the advancement of the Colony worked not for their own benefit, but for that of others. If this be true it is certainly a new feature in the plan. (Laughter.) . . . I am glad to know there is a prospect of success in the Colony. . . . I hope that the success of this Association will stir up the energies of the Government to make improvements at home. I contend that there is ground enough at home for all the people it has to support. . . . Capital does much evil as well as good. . . . Though the labourer produces wealth, the rich man puts it in his pocket. The poor labourer is left to starve." Thomas Goode continues in this strain, airing his socialistic views, till the patience of the meeting is exhausted. There are cries of "Question! Question!" "Off! Off!" and hisses. "Why, gentlemen," Thomas says, " I am ashamed of you: you put me in mind of the geese in my country."

Another person rises in the body of the hall : " I will move the adjournment of this meeting if order is not restored."

Again the pertinacious Thomas attempts to speak, but there is groaning and hooting.

The chairman rises : " It is my wish, and the wish of all connected with the management of this Association, that the freest scope should be given to every gentleman to express his opinion on the subject; and if the gentleman who is addressing the meeting will put his remarks in moderate limits, I am sure that he will be patiently attended to." (Applause.)

"Thomas Goode, of Kettering," proceeds to unburden his soul, and concludes by saying, " I have worked hard. I have a large family. We had twenty children. (Loud laughter.) If I go to Australia I will take two of them with me. I know how to plough, and to mow, and to sow, and to reap, and all other agricultural operations. Besides that I can dig, and I understand well-digging, and the feeding of pigs and poultry, and if the Colony wants such a man as me, I am the man to go."

Thomas sits down, apparently well satisfied. Whether he came to the Colony or not, history does not record.

The chairman puts the final resolution to the meeting: "That amongst the unoccupied portions of the earth which form part of the British dominions, the south coast of Australia appears to be a spot peculiarly suitable for founding a Colony." This is unanimously carried.

The labours of the South Australian Association were successful. Much credit is due to Robert Gouger, secretary of the Association, after whom one of the streets in Adelaide is named. In 1834 a Colonisation Bill passed both Houses of Parliament.

Theory is easy; practice often difficult. It is one thing to draw a plan, and quite another to make the plan effective. So the promoters of the new Colony discovered. It was probable that all their efforts would be abortive. The draughtsmen had been very exacting. One of the provisions of the Bill was that the British Government should not be in any way financially responsible. The Board of Commissioners, in whom the interests of the proposed new Colony were to be vested, had to raise the necessary funds. A large sum of money had to be borrowed;—£35,000 worth of land had to be sold before the plan could be made operative. This was the difficulty. It was not likely that shrewd capitalists would invest money in a Colony which, as yet, had no real existence. Some were afraid of a second South Sea Bubble. The land would not sell. Wreck seemed inevitable. On every hand there were rocks, and the winds were adverse. It was here that George Fife Angas—one of the Board of Commissioners—came to the rescue. To give the Colony a start he proposed the formation of a company. It was to purchase the necessary amount of land, and to send out implements and workers. The "South Australian Company" was formed; the necessary amount of capital subscribed. In this way initial difficulties were overcome, and the way was opened up for giving tangibility to the colonisation plan.

JOHN CHARLES WHITE: A PIONEER WESLEYAN LOCAL PREACHER IN SOUTH AUSTRALIA

CHAPTER III

PREPARING TO BUILD

IT is the year 1835. Sheffield, in an ecclesiastical sense, is astir. There has been a clerical invasion. Mounted on horses, by stage-coaches, and on foot, a great number of strangers have entered the town. They are cleanly shaven: rolls of white linen are round their necks; and each wears a dark coat, with a ponderous collar. They are travel-stained. The faces of many are weather-beaten. It is a gathering of Methodist preachers. They have come up to Sheffield, from all parts of the kingdom, to attend the Annual Conference. There are four hundred and eighty-eight in the town. The Napoleon-like Joseph Taylor is there, of whose preaching Adam Clarke said, " It is hot, and heavy, like a tailor's goose." The tall form of the scholarly Thomas Galland may be seen sauntering through the streets. The oldest preacher in the body, James Wood, has put in an appearance. For sixty-two years he has been a preacher in the Methodist Connexion. The erect and dignified Richard Reece is on his way to Carver Street Chapel. Robert Newton and Jabez Bunting again clasp each other by the hand. No wonder that some of the preachers look anxious, and some are sad. We see them in groups, discussing the situation. The Connexion is in a disturbed state. Methodism is being weighed in the balance. No heart is sadder than the heart of the gifted and able John Stephens. His son, Joseph Rayner, has resigned his position as a preacher, and has not "quietly withdrawn." *The Christian Advocate*, edited by another son, is blowing a militant blast. Dr. Warren has taken up arms against the Connexion. A revolutionary body has met in Sheffield to demand certain changes at the hands of the Conference. Methodism is "beset behind and before," and heavy hands are laid upon her. Is it any wonder that the minds of many of the preachers are perplexed, and their hearts sad?

The Conference is a long one. It is no time of jubilation. For twenty-one days the brethren sit in solemn conclave, and then depart.

Not many days after, another meeting, of a very different character, is held. It is not to consider questions of spiritual, but of political import. It is not to bind up the wounds of a stricken Church, but to give a new Colony a start—a Colony in which three sons of the Rev. John Stephens, to whom we have just referred, are to take a prominent part. The locality is London, and the place of meeting Exeter Hall. Colonel Torrens, M.P., is in the chair. The Duke of Wellington is not able to attend. His apology is read. There are no anxious faces here, nor sad hearts. It is a jovial gathering. A dinner is being given to Captain John Hindmarsh, R.N., whose "appointment as Governor of the new Colony of South Australia His Majesty has most graciously approved." Amongst those present is George Fife Angas,[1] to whom South Australia owes much. The "health of the Duke of Wellington, and other members of the House of Lords who supported the South

[1] See *Life of George Fife Angas*, by Edwin Hodder.

Australian Colonisation Bill," is proposed. The members who supported the Bill in the Lower House are honoured in the same way, with " three times three." It is a most enthusiastic gathering. The cheering is " immense." All present seem to be of opinion that the new Colony about to be established in South Australia will be a great success. The chairman speaks of South Australia as a land " where the climate of Paradise appears to have survived the Fall." In words, more wise, he says: " Britons cannot compel all nations to receive British goods more freely, but they can plant new nations to become customers. They can open unlimited markets in the now boundless forest. . . . In the growing markets of Australia, England will find not only increasing supplies of the most valuable materials, but also an increasing demand for her fabrics." In conclusion, he says: " The Colony of South Australia may be considered as now established. Biddings have already been made for the whole—and for more than the whole —of the land required by Act of Parliament to be disposed of before the first expedition shall depart. In a few weeks the first emigrants will be departing from these shores; they will go to eat pleasant bread in a pleasant land,—at all events the prayers of the present company will go with them. . . . Let their ways be ways of pleasantness, and all their paths be peace."

After the lapse of more than sixty years, the descendants of the first emigrants can smile at some of these post-prandial remarks. If Colonel Torrens (after whom our city river is named) had been caught in a South Australian dust-storm, or had sat in a shepherd's hut with the temperature 114 degrees in the shade, he would have had grave doubts as to whether "the climate of South Australia had survived the Fall." Probably he would think that it had come under a double curse.

But we are in Exeter Hall, sixty-three years ago. Another speaker rises. He tells the company that the first batch of emigrants are "a body of men who, in numbers, in intelligence, in respectability, in everything which constitutes religious and moral worth, far surpass any body of Englishmen who ever thought of settling in a distant Colony since the days of William Penn. . . . Gentlemen," he exclaims, "let us drink to the health, happiness, and prosperity of the emigrants to South Australia. May their community long flourish, a bright image of the moral, social, and political greatness of the parent country, unaffected by any of those evils which are inseparable from old societies."

Another speaker is Mr. John Morphett. He rose to distinction in the new land, and lived to a grand old age. The writer remembers him as a tall, aristocratic-looking man. He became President of the South Australian Legislative Council, and was knighted by the Queen. He has gone the way of all flesh, but his memory is perpetuated in Morphett Street and Morphett Vale.

He responds on behalf of the emigrants. "In heart," he says, "I am now a South Australian."

The Governor-elect is now on his feet—no ordinary man. The memory of such brings a flush of pride to the cheek, and makes an English heart, though born in Australia, beat quick. He had fought under Nelson at the Nile and Trafalgar. Such was his gallantry that Nelson summoned him to the deck, and thanked him in the presence of the officers and crew. "As Governor of South

Australia," he says, "I will continue to do my duty." The Aborigines are not forgotten. "My power as Governor," he says, "will be of little avail without being seconded by the exertions of the colonists. I therefore call upon them to second me in this good work, and, above all things, to prevent the Aborigines from imbibing from them a taste for that bane of humanity—spirituous liquors; and I consider the most effective way the colonists can do this will be by setting them an example in forming one vast temperance society."

Alas! such good advice, in relation to some of the colonists, was thrown away. The Aborigines suffered much from their contact with unprincipled and lecherous whites. They soon learned to drink, swear, gamble, and to commit baser sins. While as yet the first settlers dwelt in tents and bough-booths on the shores of Holdfast Bay, notices were fastened to the gum-trees offering a reward for information as to the persons who supplied drink to the Aborigines. To-day they are a weak, degraded, decimated race, doomed to speedy extinction.

The first batch of emigrants did not leave

England so soon as Colonel Torrens anticipated. It was not till February 1836 that the two first vessels—the *John Pirie* and the *Duke of York*—left the old land for these shores. These vessels were sent out by private enterprise. They belonged to the newly-formed South Australian Company.

PROCLAMATION TREE, HOLDFAST BAY, 1898

CHAPTER IV

LAYING THE FOUNDATIONS

BEFORE South Australia was colonised there were a few white settlers upon its shores. They lived on Kangaroo Island. It was so called by Captain Flinders, who discovered it in 1802. At that time the island was uninhabited.

About seventeen years after Flinders' visit there were at least two white men upon Kangaroo Island. How they got there we are not in a position to state. They were either escaped convicts from some of the older settlements, or runaway sailors. In course of time these were joined by others. Wild men they were—hard as the rocks; salt as the sea. Away from the restraints of civilisation they led a lawless life. The conscience was seared; the spiritual instincts blunted. Apparently, they had no higher ambition in life than to gratify their material instincts. In a spiritual sense they must have descended almost to the level of the kangaroos. Their time was spent in whaling, sealing, and wallaby hunting. Sometimes they made a trip to the mainland and stole some of the blacks. One of the early emigrants, who came by the *Africane* in 1836, has left on record a description of one of these marauders. She says: " We next proceeded around the island, and as we entered Nepean Bay the flag was hoisted and two guns fired to announce our approach. A boat, in which was a gentleman of the name of Samuel Stephens (who came out in the *Duke of York*) came off, rowed by four men, one of whom was Nathaniel Thomas, and had been resident on the island many years, but his appearance, I thought, was more like that of a savage than an Englishman. This man, by some mischance, fell overboard, and, as the tide was running strong at the time, he was carried some distance from the vessel before assistance could be rendered, and, although he could swim well enough, he was watched by those on board with considerable anxiety on account of the sharks, which were known to be numerous. An oar, however, was thrown to him, on which he got astride till the boat reached him; and when he was again on the deck he shook himself like a dog does when just out of the water, and took no more notice of the matter."[1]

Before the year 1836 these white buccaneers had a whole island to themselves. They were "monarchs of all they surveyed," their right "there was none to dispute." But a change was coming.

In 1836 a vessel hove in sight. We can imagine how curiously some of the natives on the mainland may have watched her as she mysteriously tacked along the coast of Kangaroo Island, making for Nepean Bay. At length she dropped anchor. This was on the 29th of July 1836. It was the *Duke of York*, commanded by Captain R. G. Morgan. She had brought the first contingent of emigrants to the new land. In addition to officers and sailors (who went back with the ship) there were thirteen passengers on board: nine adults and four children. As this event will ever have historical value, we give the names of the passengers: Mr.

---

[1] Diary of Mrs. Robt. Thomas, wife of first proprietor of *South Australian Register*.

Samuel Stephens (first manager of the South Australian Company); Mr. Thomas Hudson Beare, Mrs. Lucy Ann Beare, and the following four children—Lucy, Arabella, Elizabeth, and William L. Beare; also Charlotte Hudson Beare (afterwards Mrs. Samuel Stephens); and Messrs. Thomas Mitchell, Charles Powel, D. H. Schreyvogle, William West, and C. Neall. These were the pioneer settlers in South Australia—the first contingent of sinewy men and women who were to make "the parched ground a pool," and the "wilderness blossom as a rose."

Jetties, of course, there were none. The passengers would be carried "pick-a-back" by the sailors, or wade through the surf to the shore. There seems to have been some competition amongst the passengers of the *Duke of York* as to who should be the first to put foot on South Australian soil. The Captain soon settled the question. The boat was launched. "Baby Beare" was put on board. She was rowed to the beach. Amid the cheers of the emigrants one of the sailors carried her through the surf, and planted her feet on the shore.

What was the first act of the settlers on reaching shore? To go on an exploring expedition? To attend to their material wants? No. To give thanks to God. There was neither ordained preacher nor temple made with hands. In the great temple of nature, under the blue vault of heaven, they returned thanks for the mercies of the voyage. Is it not a picture worthy of the poet's muse or the painter's brush? A little band of men and women—pioneer settlers, nation builders—met on the shores of a country practically unknown. Before them is the ocean. Riding at anchor in Nepean Bay is the vessel in which they have sailed. Behind is the dense scrub of Kangaroo Island. Away in the distance the mainland, on which they will ultimately dwell. Under foot the beach of Nepean Bay. Captain Morgan stands up. The emigrants cluster around him. Heads are bowed and hearts uplifted while the Captain conducts a short service, concluding with extempore prayer. Are not these the "deeds that have won the empire"? the memory of which should never die.

After spending a few hours on shore the emigrants returned to the vessel. Here they spent the night. Next day they made preparations to build huts, and pitched their tents. It was on Kangaroo Island that the first settlement was to be formed. Such were the instructions that the South Australian Company gave to Samuel Stephens. Shops were to be erected, and cottages for shepherds and herdsmen built. This proved to be a mistake, as further on we shall see.

What a strange experience the first emigrants' must have been! How very unreal! Were they awake, or did they dream? Had they really left the Old Land? Were their loved ones the other side of the world? What a sense of loneliness at times must have come over them! They had lived in a land of villages and towns; a land where myriads hurried through the streets. Here neither street, village, nor town could be seen. It was an empty land. No street since creation had been formed, and no city built. Save the members of their own community, and a few half-savage whalers and sealers, no white face was to be seen. They had been accustomed to the roar of traffic; here, save the chatter of the birds, the sigh of the wind, or the sough of the ocean, no sounds could be heard. The solitude at times must have been oppressive; the silence intense. On the one hand, far as the eye could reach, there was interminable scrub; on the other, the trackless sea.

But there were gleams of sunshine amid the gloom. They were in a new world. Here were strange fruits and flowers, and trees that never shed their leaves. Here were peculiar insects and gaily-dressed birds. The warble of the magpie made glad the heart, and the weird laugh of the jackass first caused alarm, and then provoked a smile. They saw the wallaby hopping in the scrub; the emu running along with her chicks; and, peradventure, the well-conditioned wombat hurrying to his hole. The heart danced with delight at the sight of a sail. Ere long there was the joy of receiving a letter from "home." How firmly the precious missive would be grasped! How quickly the recipient would hurry away! The hand would tremble and the heart beat fast as the fingers tore away the seal. Ah! there was the old familiar hand, but changed. The letter was blotched and the writing blurred. Here and there was a stain.

What did it mean? A tear—a soul's travail—the liquified love of a father's or mother's heart. How fast the emigrant's eye would fly over the words till the end was reached! The nerves were steadier now. The reader would begin again. This time the eye would linger over the sentences whilst the soul listened with delight to the music of a familiar voice, and gazed in ecstasy upon a sweet but intangible face. But duty calls. The log fire must be renewed; the kettle must be hung. The letter is folded up, only to be again and again unfolded and re-read. At night the emigrant dreams. Space is annihilated. He or she is in Old England now. The snow is falling. A little cottage appears in view. There is the garden in which the honeysuckle and jessamine grow. A dear old figure is standing at the gate. A wild blast comes sweeping by. The emigrant awakes. Ah! it was only a dream—a beautiful creation shattered by the scream of an excited parrot or the howl of a hungry dingo. The soul may have seen Old England, but the body is in a tent or reed-hut on the shores of an Australian bay.

Shortly after the arrival of the *Duke of York* the

Lady Mary Pelham dropped anchor in Nepean Bay. There were six passengers on board, and twenty-three officers and men. She was soon followed by the *John Pirie*, laden with stores, carrying fourteen passengers and fourteen officers and men. All these vessels belonged to the South Australian Company. It was private enterprise that fitted them up and sent them out. No emigrant vessel despatched by the Government Commissioners had yet arrived. The *Cygnet* was the first to set sail, followed by the *Rapid*, having on board the Surveyor-General, Colonel Light.

There were two questions exercising the emigrants' minds. One was—

Where will the City be Built?

Until this question was settled nothing definite could be done. It was one in which the people had no direct voice. Sole power was vested in Colonel Light. In the way of surveying the country, of fixing the site, nothing could be decided until he came.

It was on the 19th of August 1836 that the *Rapid* rode into Nepean Bay. At once the Colonel set to work. Kangaroo Island, as a suitable place for settlement, was condemned. The land was poor. Port Lincoln could not be recommended. The waterway was not sufficiently safe. Much was to be held in favour of Holdfast Bay. The Colonel's position was a most responsible one. It was not a temporary question that he had to settle, but one the effect of which was to continue for all time. It was not for the present generation that he had to decide, but for generations unborn. Posterity must either applaud or condemn.

In fixing the site of the city several things had to be taken into consideration. So far as a mere basis on which to build is concerned, such could easily be found. It was not so easy to find a suitable port, or a stream of water from which the inhabitants could drink. It was these difficulties that Colonel Light had to face. For some time he could neither find suitable port nor stream. After a careful examination of the coast both these difficulties were met. An arm of the sea was discovered running several miles inland, offering an admirable shelter for ships.

LAYING THE FOUNDATIONS

Here the Colonel decided to fix his port. Farther inland a fresh-water river had been found, larger than any yet seen. On the banks of this stream he decided that the city should be built.

Four months had passed away since Colonel Light had begun his work. During that time several emigrant ships had arrived. As Kangaroo Island had been condemned, most of the passengers were landed at Holdfast Bay. On Christmas Day, 1836, there must have been about three hundred settlers on South Australian soil.

To every community there must be a head. It seems to be a necessity of our nature that there should be some embodiment of law and order, and in every social organism there is something lacking until that necessity is met. It was so in the experience of the early emigrants. The site for the city had been fixed, but the Governor had not yet arrived. How anxiously they looked for his advent!

WHEN WILL THE GOVERNOR COME?
would be an oft-repeated question. Frequently the eyes of the emigrant scanned the ocean. What

was the reason of the delay? At length another sail hove in sight. It was the long-expected and anxiously-looked for H.M.S. *Buffalo*. It had the Governor on board, the Resident Commissioner, J. H. Fisher, and the Colonial Chaplain, the Rev. C. B. Howard. What excitement there must have been amongst the emigrants! What demonstrations of joy! Rush-huts and tents would be vacated. Down the emigrants would run, young and old, to the edge of the water. What a motley assemblage! The tall hat would be in evidence, so would the smock-frock and gaiters. The Governor and party would either have to submit to the orthodox style of transhipment—" pick-a-back"—or take off boots and socks, and wade through the water. The position may not have been a very dignified one, but necessity knows no law, and is no respecter of persons. The Governor was received by the leading men of the small community. There was a preliminary meeting in the tent of Robert Gouger, Colonial Secretary. An adjournment was then made to a large gum-tree. The Proclamation was read! The British flag unfurled! A royal salute was fired! The air rang with hurrahs! A cold lunch, consisting chiefly of cold pork and a ham, was served up in a very primitive style. The Governor mounted a chair, and gave the first toast, "The King," which was received with "three times three." The national anthem followed. Other toasts were given. "Rule, Britannia" was sung. The emigrants were well-nigh wild with joy, and the shades of evening brought to a close the most exciting day (save the day of their landing) that they had seen. Is it any wonder that the children of the first emigrants, to this day, on the anniversary of the Colony, travel to Holdfast Bay in tens of thousands, where patriotic speeches are still delivered, old colonists are honoured, and royal salutes fired?

In the Governor's Proclamation the spirit in which English people set about the work of colonisation, and the basis on which they build, are to be seen:—

In announcing to the colonists of His Majesty's province of South Australia, the establishment of the Government, I hereby call upon them to conduct themselves, on all occasions, with order and quietness, duly to respect the laws, and, by a course of industry and sobriety, by the practice of sound morality, and a strict observance of the ordinances of religion, to prove themselves worthy to be the founders of a great and free Colony.

The Proclamation also stated that the Governor would take every lawful means to secure to the Aborigines all the rights of British subjects.

The foundations were now well and truly laid. How the superstructure was reared we must leave for the next chapter.

WESLEYAN PLAN FOR THE ADELAIDE CIRCUIT.

No. 1.

SOUTH AUSTRALIA.

PLACES.	TIME	MAY 27	JUNE 3	JUNE 10	JUNE 17	JUNE 24	JULY 1	JULY 8	JULY 15	JULY 22	JULY 29	AUGUST 5	AUGUST 12	AUGUST 19	AUGUST 26	SEPTEMBER 2	SEPTEMBER 9	SEPTEMBER 16	SEPTEMBER 23
CHAPEL	10	6	1	2	5	3	1	7	2	8	3	2	6	5	7	3	1	2	7
DITTO	3	3	2	8	1	5	7	8	3	5	1	7	7	3	3	6	2	6	1
DITTO	6	7	2L	3	6	SW	3	6	1	7	6	5	3	8	2	6	3	5	2
DITTO, WEDNESDAY EVENING	½6	8	6	7	1	4	8	2	3	6	1	8	1	7	6	2	7	3	5
FORBES SQUARE	½2	2	4	5	3	7	6	6	5	3	2	7	3	6	1	4	6	2	6

PREACHERS.
1 WHITE
2 ABBOTT
3 MINOHAM
4 LILLYWAPP
5 SPARSHOTT

ON TRIAL.
6 SLEEP
7 BREEZE
8 TURNER

Reference.....L.—Lovefeast.....W.—Watchnight.

PRINTED BY A. MACDOUGALL, RUNDLE-STREET, ADELAIDE.

ADELAIDE: HINDLEY STREET IN 1846

CHAPTER V

RAISING THE SUPERSTRUCTURE

THE foundations of the Colony had been laid, now came the work of raising the superstructure.

Of the present generation of South Australians it may be said: "Other men laboured, and ye have entered into their labours." In building up the Commonwealth it was under peculiar conditions that the pioneers had to work. Says one of the most worthy of them: "Men generally laboured from early morn till dusky eve. Restless nights were frequent, and hard work by day caused us often to feel weary by the way." Yet there were compensations. As we shall see, there was a great deal of romance about those early days that is no longer possible. If colonists are more comfortable to-day, their circumstances are more prosaic.

We saw that the first temporary settlement was at Kangaroo Island, the second at Holdfast Bay.

Here the emigrants dwelt in tents, and rude huts made of rushes and boughs. "Hutting" themselves was the term they used. Some, for the first evening or two after their arrival, had to sleep in the open air. They made for themselves beds among the bushes on the beach, just above high-water mark. One of the pioneers, who arrived on a Saturday, in January 1837, tells how himself, wife, and two children had to camp in the open air from Saturday night to Monday morning. They then set to work, cutting down trees, and covering them with bushes. In this way (as many others did) they constructed a temporary shelter. The life was rough, but it was romantic. One is reminded of the Feast of Tabernacles, when the Children of Israel dwelt in booths made of boughs. Gentle folk and simple folk, learned and illiterate, dwelt together as one family.

One of the pioneers (Mrs. Robert Thomas) has

left on record a description as to how the emigrants spent their first Christmas far away from the "dear Old Land." In her diary she writes: "December the 25th, 1836. This being Christmas Day, and Sunday, divine service was held for the first time in the hut of the principal surveyor, a short distance from our tents. We attended, taking our seats with us; the signal for assembling being the firing of a gun. The congregation numbered twenty-five persons, including the two gentlemen who conducted the service, the thermometer standing at 100 degrees, and most of those assembled being in the open air. . . . We kept up the old custom of Christmas as far as having a plum-pudding for dinner was concerned, likewise a ham, and a parrot pie, but one of our neighbours, as we afterwards found, had a large piece of roast beef, though we were not aware, at the time, that any fresh meat was to be had in the Colony."

Hereby hangs a tale. Where the roast beef came from was at first a mystery. It gives point to the old proverb, "It is an ill wind that blows nobody any good." It appears that the captain of one of the emigrant vessels (the *Africane*) had a cow and a calf on board. Whilst the vessel was lying at anchor, for change of scenery and food the cow and calf were transhipped to land. They were placed under the care of one of the emigrants. Unfortunately in one respect, and fortunately in another, the cow was tied to a tree not far from a lagoon. She got over the bank, fell in, and was so much injured that death had to be decreed. She was killed. In this way some of the emigrants were supplied with a little Christmas beef.

There is one sentence in Mrs. Thomas' diary that is very suggestive: they went to the rush-hut of the principal surveyor for divine service, "taking their seats with them." Comment is not necessary. Two laymen conducted the service, because no minister of the gospel had yet arrived.

From the letter of another lady pioneer [1] we got a very good idea of the pioneer settlement at Holdfast Bay, the settlers, and their surroundings: "The beach is a very fine white sand, hard close to the water, and then rises to hillocks of deep loose sand, with shrubs growing in it. When

[1] Miss Chauncey, published by the *South Australian Advertiser*.

we had passed these little banks of sand, which do not extend above a quarter of a mile, we entered a fine open plain, with beautiful trees scattered over it, looking very green, also some shrubs, although at the end of a hot summer. The stores, and a few huts and tents, are erected at the entrance of the plain, and we walked on about three-quarters of a mile, to where many of the settlers had pitched their tents. It appeared like a beautiful park. Some of the trees were large and old. They were chiefly the she-oak, and tea-tree, and gum, and several others we did not know. There were wild strawberries, raspberries, and a sort of cranberry. The kangaroos are scarce, and some have been sold at one shilling a pound. We saw flocks of green and crimson parrots. They were plentiful, and very good eating; also the bronze-winged pigeon; cockatoos—black and crimson, and white and yellow. The natives eat rats, snakes, or anything they can find. They will come to shake hands very friendly. They ask for biscuit, and say 'good-night,' which they know to be a sort of salutation, so say it any time. There was a woman buried last night who came in the *Coro-*

mandel. A party of natives attended, and seemed very much affected, putting up their hands; and an old man whom they called Ginykin—their chief, we think—wept. They are very superstitious and very idle, lying under a tree all day; but in the evening they have a dance, or merry-making they call 'corrobery.' One of the first things we noticed, on entering the settlement, was the truly English custom: I mean several printed bills—one a caution, the other a reward. The caution was a high fine on any person found giving spirits or wine to the natives; the reward was £5 for the discovery of a person who had already transgressed the orders. There were several others posted about on the gum-trees. . . . There was a dance in the evening, under a large tent, or rather made of one of the sails of the ship, which Captain Chesser put up for the purpose of inviting *Coromandel* emigrants from 'Coromandel village,' as they call the assemblage of (tents) they are in, till the wooden ones are built in Adelaide. . . . We all rose early, with parrots chirping over our heads, and breakfasted with Mrs. Brown. The coffee mill is nailed to a tree outside the tent, and the roaster stands close by the side. The fire for cooking is on the ground close by. The fresh branches of gum-trees burn like dry wood; firing will cost us nothing for many years. Each family has erected a tent under a tree, and dug a well by the side of it. . . . Water can be had for digging about six feet—all over the plains, called Glenelg. . . . The trees are generally from fifty to a few hundred feet apart, and mostly without any bush between." The above are the first impressions of one of the early emigrants, who was evidently of a very observing turn of mind.

The romance was not all joyous. One of the first settlers complained of the fleas in the sand hills, and the mosquitoes, no doubt attracted by the lagoons. The ubiquitous rat had also made its appearance, and was making inroads on scanty stores.

After the site for the city had been fixed, a move was made from the temporary settlement on the coast to the environs of the prospective town. There were neither roads nor conveyances. The emigrants had to walk through the woods to the city site (a distance of about seven miles), and transport their possessions as best they could. Some were fortunate enough to secure the services of a small hand-cart. Some had to carry furniture, as well as children, in their arms.

The land on which the city was to be built not yet being available, another temporary encampment was formed. The locality was the banks of the Torrens, between what is now called North Terrace and the river.

The settlers had few of the advantages of civilisation. There was neither slate, shingle, board, nor galvanised iron depôt. Some of the huts were composed of mud and grass, covered with reeds; others were wooden frames on which canvas was stretched. "Government House"—the "Vice-Regal Mansion," as it was sarcastically called—was a wattle and daub hut. In wet weather it was a difficult matter to keep rain out. The "hut-wife" had to resort to various expedients. Sometimes umbrellas were propped up to keep goods dry.

Some of the emigrants, before leaving England, had made arrangements for a few small houses, ready made, to be shipped. They were to come by the *Tam o' Shanter*. Unfortunately, as the vessel was sailing from Kangaroo Island to what is known as Port Adelaide, she struck on a sand bar, and had to remain there some time. Says one of the pioneers: "The sailors had to attend to the ship, and we had to do as best we could. Some cut down a few light saplings, and, putting them together as well as they were able, went down into the bed of the river, and cut some grass with which to make a kind of wurley hut, into which we had to go, and there spend the winter, improving the place a little as the days went by." We were "frequently obliged to fix up umbrellas, etc., to keep off the drenching rain, no other means being available at the time."

These privations were not without their advantages. They developed thrift, determination, self-reliance. The early settlers did not "run to the Government" when they wanted a bed or a new broom. Tradition says there was a time when the Government Treasury contained but eighteenpence.

One who came to the Colony in the early days, and who published his reminiscences at "home," thus describes the temporary settlement on the banks of the Torrens: "The huts were scattered about without any attempt at regularity or uniformity. Every man had built his house on the spot where whim or choice pointed out, or where material was easiest got; the consequence was, that a collection of as primitive-looking wigwams as can be well imagined soon lined the banks of the Torrens—some of them facing the east, some the west; in fact, every point of the compass might have claimed one or more facing it. They stood just as though a mad bull had been playing his antics among them, and had tossed them hither and thither. Nor was the appearance of the dwellings less amusing or extraordinary than their general positions. Most of them possessed an aperture to afford egress and ingress; but few, if any, could boast of a window of any kind. A fireplace was not deemed essential, though several had an opening at one end, surmounted by an empty pork cask deprived of the ends, to serve as a chimney. A great portion of the emigrants, however, contented themselves without a fire, except outside, where it might be seen blazing, with a pot hung over it *à la* gipsy." An old colonist (J. W. Bull) says: "It was not an unusual thing, in hot or showery weather, to see a lady watching a kettle or camp-oven under an umbrella."

Here and there, in the temporary encampment that we have described, there was some little attempt at order. It was only natural that emigrants who came out in the same ship would desire to pitch their tents or to build their huts together; so in the fugitive settlement on the banks of the Torrens there was a "Buffalo Row" and a "Coromandel Row." Evidently, the emigrants who had come by the *Buffalo* and the *Coromandel* had pitched their tents in a line together. "Buffalo Row" stood between the Torrens and the present site of Trinity Church; "Coromandel Row" a little eastward.

There was a great deal of romance about these far-off times. Everything was new. There was no snobbery. The settlers led a free, unconventional kind of life. Servants were difficult to get. Those who came out soon got married. Ladies had to do what is termed menial work. A pork barrel, end up, or a packing case, served as a table; boxes and trunks did duty as seats; rushes made a comfortable bed. Tin pannikins were used for tea. Ship's biscuit and salt pork was the staple food. Sometimes there was a welcome variety in the form of wallaby or native birds. The settlers had their social gatherings in tents and huts. The red-letter days were the days when a letter was received from "home," or an emigrant vessel came in. After a short time the "first-comers" were amused by seeing "new chums" marching up to the settlement with guns over their shoulders and pistols in their belts. Says one of our lady pioneers: "The few people here were like a happy family out for a lengthened picnic. . . . No person arriving now can form any idea of the life of the early settlers. It was sometimes very hard to forget all that we had left in the old country, and particularly friends, and to determine to make the best of our surroundings; but all managed to put up with the roughness, and be contented. Happily, there was scarcely any sickness in the population. No false shame troubled us. If friends came in they were welcome. We might be ironing, cooking, or working at any menial occupation, and it made the occupation pleasanter to have a friend to chat to. The first wedding I attended was in winter. It being too muddy to walk, we went in a bullock-dray. . . . No one appeared to fear for the future, although, of course, no one could anticipate what the future might bring forth."

Judging from some of the letters written home by the emigrants, they seemed to be quite satisfied with their lot. The following is a copy of one :—

To——
 I write to you according to promise, hoping, at the same time, yourself, wife, and children are well, as we are at present. I did not write before, for I wished to send you some particulars of the place. We sailed from England the 25th of September 1837, and had a most beautiful voyage, for we could have come the whole distance in a longboat. We were four months on our passage. . . . This is one of the loveliest countries ever seen. The town is on a rising ground about seven miles from the sea, . . . with high mountains in the rear. It is a lovely black soil, and capable of producing anything. The trees are green the whole year. Things grow here with astonishing rapidity, and finer than ever were seen in England. The Colony is increasing very fast, and all manner of trade is flourishing, especially the builders'. . . . John, if you were out here you would do well, for you could start in business for yourself. . . . This is the land of plenty. A steady man, who is industrious, in a few years may make a comfortable fortune. . . . I should like very much to see you out here. . . . Come as soon as you can, for the early-comers get the best chance.

No wonder that there was a fascination for English folk about letters like this, especially when they were garnished with references to blackfellows, kangaroos, and emus. The "comfortable fortune," of which the emigrant above quoted speaks, was more imaginary than real.

After Colonel Light had fixed the site for the city there was considerable dispute. Some wanted it in one place, and some in another. Governor Hindmarsh was pleased with the surroundings, but thought that the city would be too far from the harbour. He expressed a preference for Encounter Bay. Fortunately, Colonel Light's power in the matter was absolute. He manfully stood his ground. Experience has demonstrated the wisdom of his choice. A more suitable site for the city (after more than sixty years' experience) it would be difficult to find. It was within easy reach of the sea, and was surrounded by good country, and on rising ground. There was fresh water in the Torrens, and the eastern hills formed a beautiful background. Some of the descendants of the pioneers may imagine that the city site and its environs were densely covered with scrub. Such was not the case. To the north the country was open. There were belts of gums lining watercourses. To the south the country was well wooded, in many places resembling an English park.[1] Fifty years after the site for the city had been fixed, when celebrating the Colony's Jubilee (1886), Sir Henry Ayers, one of the most worthy of the old colonists, said: "Can any one at this time, after fifty years' experience, and with all the knowledge possessed of our extensive seaboard, point out any other site so well adapted in all respects, or indeed approaching the suitableness of the one chosen? Harassed and annoyed by the interference of some, and the criticisms of others, Colonel Light . . . fearlessly acted on his own good judgment, leaving it, as he said, to posterity to decide whether I am entitled 'to praise or blame.' Posterity speaks out to-night, as succeeding genera-

---

[1] The nature of some of the suburban country is evident from the names given to it by the early emigrants: "Goodwood Park," "Unley Park," "Black Forest." These places have lost their park-like appearance, but the writer, as a lad, roamed over them when they were studded with trees. The picture, "A Primitive Australian Scene," will give the reader some idea of the virgin character of the country on which Adelaide and suburbs are now built.

tions will through all time to come, loudly in praise of the man who, by the exercise of his ability, was indeed the founder of Adelaide, and whose dying wish to be so regarded has been so singularly fulfilled."

The same wisdom displayed in the choice of the city site was manifested in laying it out. The city lies foursquare. Provision was made for wide streets, public squares, and a park around the town. At the request of King William IV. it was called "Adelaide," in honour of the Royal Consort. In his important work Colonel Light was ably assisted by the Deputy-Surveyor, George S. Kingston (afterwards Sir George), father of the present Premier of South Australia. The Colonel's life in the Colony soon came to a close. Hard work and worry undermined his constitution. He died of consumption in 1839. His heart was always in the city, and his body is buried in one of its squares. A monument marks his resting-place. No such monument, however, is necessary. From the top of the Post Office tower to-day a vaster monument—the creation of his genius—may be seen.

To the new Colony the dark figure of dissension came. It appeared in official circles. There were disputes between Governor Hindmarsh and Colonel Light over the city site. There was some wrangling over the naming of the squares and the streets.[1] In a previous chapter we stated that the interests of the Colony were vested in Commissioners appointed by the Crown. A Resident Commissioner was sent out. This dual arrangement—Resident Commissioner and a Governor—did not succeed. It led to divided authority. They came into conflict. The result was, that before Governor Hindmarsh had spent two years in the Colony he was recalled. On the whole, he had served the Colony well. He made himself one with the people, and was highly esteemed. His farewell words recall the lofty tone of his Proclamation: "If the colonists do themselves justice; if they respect the laws, and attend to the ordinances of religion; if they continue the same habits of temperance and industry which have so happily prevailed, South Australia must . . . realise the most

---

[1] The main streets and squares are named after men who took an active part in founding the Colony.

ardent wishes of its friends, and acquire, in a few years, a rank among the provinces of the British Crown without example in colonial history."

The next representative of the Crown to take up his residence at "Government Hut"—still a mud cottage—was Colonel George Gawler. He had been in the Peninsular Campaign, in which he was wounded, and had fought with great gallantry under Wellington at Waterloo. He arrived on the 12th of October 1838. The Colony had now to pass through a very critical time. Various causes contributed to this: the tide of emigration was too strong; the money received by sale of public lands was not employed in reproductive works; the Colony was ruled by a body of Commissioners the other side of the world. In spite of depression, great improvements were made. The city and Colony grew. Huts were superseded by well-built houses, bridges were constructed, and macadamised roads made.

These improvements were made in the face of great difficulties and dangers. A great deal of labour had to be spent in clearing ground. The means of transit were slow, and very defective.

Nature was not always propitious. The blacks were often a source of trouble, and so were a class of men termed "Bushrangers." These were desperate dare-devil fellows. Some of them were ticket-of-leave men, or convicts who had escaped from some of the older settlements. They were handy with firearms, and sometimes were well mounted on stolen horses. They "stuck up" travellers and out-stations. They made raids upon horses and cattle. Sometimes, under the cover of night, they would visit the city, and commit depredations. "Bail up!" was the demand, enforced at the point of a pistol. There was nothing to do but to surrender. Their rendezvous, near Adelaide, was the "tiers" in the hills. Here they lurked in densely-wooded and almost inaccessible gullies. They knew the country well, and police, in the early days, trying to thread their way through the "tiers," would be at the bushrangers' mercy.

Fortunately, in those early days, there were two or three police officers as bold as lions. Two of them deserve special mention. Their names were Alexander Tolmer and Henry Alford. They passed through some thrilling experiences. In his *Reminiscences of an Adventurous and Chequered Career*, Alexander Tolmer describes how himself and others captured a party of bushrangers on Kangaroo Island. They were living in the bush, in a wurley, some blacks being with them. "Having obtained all the necessary information I required respecting the kind of wurley, its position and surroundings, and it being dark, we again moved forward cautiously, to avoid stepping on any dry twig, for fear of giving an alarm, by which means we reached within twenty yards of the camp, and heard the men laughing and talking. Considering the position of the open wurley, the darkness of the night, and the dense scrub that surrounded the place, I deemed it expedient, upon reflection, to defer the capture until morning, which would give us a better chance of success, and accordingly made a sign to the police and our guides to fall back, and we then retraced our steps to where we had left our blankets, etc., under a bush, and there passed a wretched anxious night, supperless and without fire, the only solace being our pipes. At dawn we again approached the camp of the ruffians with cat-like silence, and, when near enough, crouched behind a bush—not a moment too soon, however, as one of the fellows got up and threw a log on the fire. After waiting until everything was silent, we once more moved forward, and then rushed simultaneously upon the fellows. They struggled desperately, however, and endeavoured to get possession of their weapons; but we were too nimble for them, and soon had them secured and handcuffed. They turned out to be two men of the 50th Regiment who were transported to Van Diemen's Land, and made their escape from the *Vixen*. Our approach to the wurley was so noiseless that the pack of fierce kangaroo dogs (twelve in number) did not hear us; but when we rushed in they commenced such a furious barking, that, added to the screaming of the native women, the imprecations and deep anathemas of the convicts, the noise was perfectly deafening."

The financial position of the Colony, during Governor Gawler's term, became so depressed that he was recalled. His expenditure may have been lavish, but he was an able and energetic officer, beloved by the people. Out of their reduced

GOVERNMENT HOUSE, ADELAIDE, IN 1846

resources the colonists contributed £500 as a testimonial. Such was Colonel Gawler's regard for the Colony, and faith in it, that he left the sum to be invested in land on his own account.

Captain George Grey (afterwards Sir George) took up his residence at what was now "Government House." During his administration—wise and effective as it was—the Colony reached its lowest ebb. A policy of retrenchment was put into practice. Valuable mines were discovered. The British Government came to the rescue. A tide of prosperity set in. The success of the Colony was assured. It had now—at the close of Governor Grey's term—been established nine years.

REV. JOHN STEPHENS

CHAPTER VI

THREE BUILDERS OF METHODIST FAME

THE year 1827 was an eventful one in Methodist history. In the nation at large a revolutionary spirit prevailed. There was a tendency to defy law, and to set at nought authority.

A revolutionary spirit is contagious. Its influence cannot be restricted. All institutions, more or less, are affected. It creeps into Church as well as into State. It demands ecclesiastical as well as political change. It was so in connection with the Methodist Church in the year 1827. A lawless spirit—a spirit that resented authority—had crept into the Connexion. The erection of an organ in one of the large chapels of Leeds, sanctioned by the Conference, was made the pretext for a rebellion. The characters of noted

Methodist ministers were traduced. A secession took place. The malcontents boasted that they had taken away, from the Leeds societies alone, "twenty-eight local preachers, seven exhorters, fifty-six leaders, and nine hundred members."

It was fortunate that the Conference of 1827 had a strong man in the chair—one who stood at least on a par with any of his illustrious predecessors. John Stephens had been elected President. "A noble person: fine temper; superior mind; an excellent preacher"; such was his character as given by a contemporary. John Stephens was born in Cornwall. He had great natural ability. From a youthful miner he became a distinguished preacher, had charge of some of the most important Circuits, and, in 1827, was elected President of the Conference.

This was the man who had to deal with the Leeds secession. He did so in a very effective manner. In an address, delivered at Leeds, speaking of the leading spirits in the unhappy division, he said: "Would to God that I could have introduced these persons to the deathbed of an old friend of mine, who got to heaven by the skin of his teeth. He had been an active agent in a division in a certain town; and, soon after the separation, he found that he could not have everything his own way because they all wanted to be masters. His head was sick, and his heart faint; and he begged permission to return to the old Connexion. He was received; but he never lifted up his head again among his brethren with confidence. God had forgiven him, but he never could forgive himself. 'Oh, sir!' said he, 'I was instrumental in taking away two or three hundred souls, but I could not keep them together; they were therefore turned adrift, and many of them got into the world. When I think of these souls my heart is almost fit to break.' This man came to his deathbed. It fell to my lot, as it accorded with my inclination, to visit him. The blood of souls was in his skirts, and he sank deeper and deeper into despair. . . . I talked with him, and prayed with him; but the heavens were as brass. . . . It seemed as if God had shut up His bowels of tender mercy against him. He continued so till near midnight, when one glimmering ray of light darted into his mind. . . . The little ray brightened into a flood of light, and the next day he died happy in God."[1]

In view of the story that we have to tell, these eloquent words have increased pathos.

Three sons of this "remarkable man" (as Dr. Smith terms him) in the early days came to South Australia. Their names were Samuel, John, and Edward. In different ways they helped to lay the foundations of the Colony. Samuel represented the pastoral and agricultural interests; John, the press; and Edward, commerce.

SAMUEL STEPHENS

Samuel Stephens was the first adult colonist to put his foot on South Australian soil. He came, as we have seen, by the *Duke of York* in 1836, and landed at Kangaroo Island. On the voyage out, service was conducted by him each Sunday, and on Wednesday evenings. He was sent out by the South Australian Company as its first manager, and was the leading spirit at the Kangaroo Island settlement.

Samuel Stephens married Miss Charlotte Hudson

[1] Smith's *History of Methodism*.

Beare, a fellow-passenger. In this way he became related to Mr. William L. Beare, who, as a lad, came out in the same vessel, and who "continues to this day."

Every detail in relation to the pioneers and their mode of life is of value, and will become increasingly so as the years roll by.

From the letters of early emigrants we get glimpses of the son of the Rev. John Stephens and his new surroundings. Under the guidance of these we see several tents and rude huts not far from the beach at Nepean Bay, Kangaroo Island. A number of people are moving about the beach, some dressed in smock-frocks and gaiters. A boat is being rowed from an emigrant vessel to the shore. Presently depth of water fails. The passengers are either carried by the sailors or wade through the water to the beach. They are met by Samuel Stephens, and conducted to his tent. Lunch is prepared. He takes them to see the site on which his cottage is to be built. It is on a gentle slope. In the foreground there are native shrubs almost down to the water's edge, and a fine view of the ocean. There are several Cashmere goats, imported by the South Australian Company, browsing the herbage. Some poultry are busy examining the nature of the new country. Cattle there is none. Mr. Stephens and his party go for a short walk in the bush. They come to a piece of land that has been cleared. It is a burial-ground. Already there are two graves in it. How very suggestive! What a lesson it reads in human mortality! How soon the most recent and smallest community needs a cemetery! As soon as we provide homes for the living, a place must be prepared for the dead. The party walk back to the beach, gathering shells and sponges. Farewell words are spoken. The visitors take their seats in the boat. Samuel Stephens goes back to his tent; while the sailors pull for the emigrant vessel, whose destination is Holdfast Bay.

After Colonel Light had pronounced against Kangaroo Island as a place of settlement, Samuel Stephens and other settlers removed to the mainland. He imported the first horse into the new Colony. One of the pioneers (Jacob Abbott), who will occupy a prominent position in these pages, describes his first meeting with the horse and its owner. Samuel Stephens was walking down the North Terrace of the embryo city, leading his newly-imported horse. A short distance away was a group of blackfellows. Directly they caught sight of the animal "their expressions of astonishment and horror were indescribable." The men shouted! The lubras screamed! The children sought refuge behind their parents. Gradually they became calmer, muttering, "Big kangaroo! Oh, big kangaroo!"

Alas! the noble-spirited Samuel Stephens soon came to an untimely end. About 1840 (four years after his arrival in the Colony), riding down one of the hills between Mount Barker and Adelaide, his horse fell. The rider was thrown; picked up in an unconscious state; and died a few hours later. He was esteemed by all, and general regret was felt among the emigrants. He has been described to the writer as "a perfect gentleman and model husband." His remains lie (far from the burial-place of his honoured father) in the West Terrace Cemetery, Adelaide.

It was Samuel Stephens who granted the use of the South Australian Company's store for the first Methodist service conducted on Kangaroo Island. Shortly afterwards his name appears as contributing two guineas towards the erection of the first Methodist chapel in Hindley Street, Adelaide. These are the only references that we can find to him in connection with Methodism in this Colony.

JOSEPH RAYNER STEPHENS

Before dealing with John Stephens, passing reference must be made to his brother, Joseph Rayner. Though he did not come to this Colony, yet indirectly he had some connection with it. Strange that a father, who apparently was conservative in his instincts, should have at least two sons who became ultra-radical. The President, who had to deal with the unhappy strife at Leeds, had the mortification, a few years later, of seeing two of his sons in a position of antagonism to the Connexion.

Like his father, Joseph Rayner Stephens was a man of great ability — energetic and eloquent. He was received on trial in 1825. In 1832 he was appointed to Ashton-under-Lyne. Here a society was formed to agitate for the disestablishment of the Church of England. The young Methodist preacher was asked to give the movement his sympathy and support. To this he consented. At the inaugural meeting a very able address was delivered by him in favour of Disestablishment. He went further, taking an official position in connection with the society, and giving the weight of his energy and ability to secure the end for which it had been formed.

To say the least, his action was unwise and unfortunate. It had a tendency to stir up strife and division. The Methodist Church, as a body, was not unfriendly to the Establishment. There was a tacit understanding that Methodist preachers would not ally themselves to the movement for separation. Complaints were made to the Chairman of the District (Robert Newton). The case was tried at the District Meeting. Joseph Rayner Stephens was requested to resign his position as secretary of the Church Separation Society, and to cease working in its interests. The verdict of the District Meeting was supported by the Conference. Not willing to give the pledge, Mr. Stephens retired from the Connexion.

The preceding sketch brings John Stephens, who took a prominent part in the founding of South Australia, on the scene.

In Chapter III. reference was made to the *Christian Advocate* and its editor. That editor was John Stephens, so named after his illustrious father.

Originally the *Christian Advocate* claimed to be a Methodist paper, though not officially connected with the Conference. Some of the leading preachers wrote for it. The editor became enamoured of the radical spirit of the times. Multitudes read the paper. Dr. Smith (no mean authority) says: "The paper was conducted with ability. Its articles were exceedingly plausible; and, in the absence of any counteracting agency, few were able to detect its fallacies." It sat in severe editorial judgment upon Dr. Bunting. It is only fair to say that it dealt out to other religious bodies that incurred its displeasure much the same treatment that was meted to Methodism. The paper was condemned by the Conference of

1833, and the discussion that took place has been put on record: "Theophilus Lessey spoke with great ability against the course pursued by the *Christian Advocate*. William Atherton, in very strong terms, condemned the conduct of those preachers who wrote for it. George Marsden reminded preachers who contributed to its columns that their writings were frequently read in pot-houses by drunkards and scoffers. James Dixon spoke of Dr. Bunting as being too great to be injured by things so little; yet his happiness might be affected by it, and the Conference ought to express some censure upon the paper. Richard Reece expressed the hope that all the preachers who had in any way given their names to the support of the paper would withdraw them."[1] These critics were some of the most eminent men in the Conference. Such sweeping condemnation would neither curb the impetuous spirit of the editor, nor make the tone of his articles less acrid.

The judgment of the Conference on the "Joseph Rayner Stephens Case" added fuel to editorial

[1] Dr. Smith's *History of Methodism*.

fire. Under the impression that his brother Joseph had a grievance, John Stephens took up the cudgels on his behalf. He was a hard hitter, and, Methodist history says, sometimes very unfair. We state the case in the most charitable way. Dr. Smith says: "The *Christian Advocate*, impelled alike by the principles that it had adopted, and the interest that the editor felt in his brother, exerted its utmost influence to rouse the members of the Methodist Society to rebellion." He further says that the members and congregations who were influenced by the paper were "beyond calculation."

The paper took a prominent part in the "Warrenite Agitation," after which both it and editor pass away from view.

It is in connection with the founding of South Australia that John Stephens somewhat abruptly rises again. That he was known to George Fife Angas, one of the founders of this Colony, is evident from a passage in Mr. Angas' published life. He says: "I went over to Blackfriars to see John Stephens."

The next we meet with him is in connection

with the publication of a book. The title is *The Land of Promise*. It was written in the interests of the new Colony of South Australia, and published in 1838. A second edition was soon called for, and published under the title of *The Rise and Progress of South Australia*. A copy of this edition the writer has been privileged to see. It consists of more than two hundred pages, and reveals considerable literary instinct.

In 1843 John Stephens is in Adelaide. He established the Adelaide *Observer*. Later on, the *Register* came into his hands. The same characteristics that were so marked in England were manifested here. He was an Ishmaelite indeed. By the courtesy of the present proprietors of the *Register*, the writer has been able to glean the following respecting his colonial career:—He " had great difficulties with his literary business, as he wielded a trenchant pen, and enemies rose up all round him, some of whom sought redress for their imagined wrongs at the hands of the law. At the time of his death his name had appeared nine times in the Cause List of the Supreme Court as defendant in libel actions." Many advertisements were withdrawn from his paper. He is represented as having "decision of character, indomitable pluck, and untiring energy in an eminent degree." He was a staunch teetotaler. In the various actions that were brought against him, it was his conviction that he suffered for righteousness' sake. One who knew him well in South Australia has left on record the following:—"He was the unflinching and unvarying advocate of civil and religious liberty; the truthful and uncompromising exposer of every proved corruption and abuse." It is probable that this free Colony to-day owes much to the powerful pen of John Stephens. He died in 1850. A contemporary says: "The victim of the severity of his own discipline and labour, but not until he had established, on a permanent basis, the reputation and success of the *Register*." Business worries, and the death of a beloved son, helped to break him down.

His portrait, in oils, hangs in the library of the *Register* office. The face is a striking one, animated and intellectual. It gives the impression of a man surcharged with nervous energy.

What a remarkable career! All that is mortal of John Stephens,—once editor of the *Christian Advocate*—the man who moved multitudes—who sat in bitter editorial judgment upon Jabez Bunting, Robert Newton, and other eminent ministers of the Methodist Connexion—the brother of Joseph Rayner Stephens, and son of one of the ablest men who sat in the chair of the British Conference,—all that is mortal of this remarkable man lies, with the remains of his brother Samuel, in the West Terrace Cemetery, Adelaide, South Australia.

The stone that marks his resting-place is wasting away. Some of the letters are obliterated. The curator of the cemetery went to considerable trouble to decipher the inscription. The following is a copy:—

In Memory of
JOHN STEPHENS,
who died
November 28th, 1850,
Aged 44 Years.

———

The memory of his worth shall never cease,
Upright in all his ways: his end was peace;
But though sincere, affectionate, and just,
His Saviour's merits were his only trust.

Of his early history in England we are not in a position to speak. We believe that he came to this Colony from Hull.

Joseph and John Stephens forsook the Church of their fathers. Edward carried his Methodism over the sea, and, as the next chapter will show, was a powerful factor in laying the foundations of a great and influential Church. He was an early emigrant. Samuel came by the first vessel, in 1836. Edward and his wife arrived by the *Coromandel* about five months later. He came to the Colony as cashier and accountant of the South Australian Company's Bank, bringing with him a portable banking-house and iron chests. When he arrived the site for the city had not been fixed, consequently he had to take up his abode in a tent, not far from the beach, at Holdfast Bay. From a private letter, written by a niece of Mrs. Edward Stephens, and published in the *Methodist Recorder* (20th January 1898), we take the following:—

I remember Aunt Stephens telling me that she and her husband went out in the second ship of emigrants:[1] he in charge of the first gold for the currency of the new Colony. They took out a house with them; that is to say, the material for a house ready prepared. But it was so difficult to fix a site for the town (afterwards Adelaide), that the material lay on the shore until at last it became unsuitable. . . . Meanwhile a camp of tents was formed, and, as theirs was the largest tent, service was held in it every Sunday. Aunt used to describe the pretty sight,—the settlers wending their way, at the sound of the bell, from the long line of tents, and under the green trees, to morning service.

Also, I remember her speaking of those most anxious days when her husband was away prospecting for a suitable site for the new town, and rumours were brought to the camp from time to time of the dark deeds of the natives, and how often she sank upon the chests containing the gold in fear and trembling, lest a raid upon the treasure in her husband's absence should be made.

We may remark, in passing, that Mrs. Stephens' fears respecting the natives were not groundless. About three years after the arrival of Mr. and Mrs. Stephens, tidings were conveyed to Adelaide that a number of white people, who had escaped from a wreck, had been murdered by the blacks. The wreck had occurred on the coast, near Lacepede

---

[1] Here there is a slight error. The *Coromandel*, in which Mr. and Mrs. Stephens sailed, was not the second ship.

Bay. The country at this time was little known. However, under instructions from the Government, a search-party was organised, amongst whom were three blacks of Encounter Bay. The country was scoured, and a ghastly discovery made. Partially covered with sand, the party found legs, arms, and other portions of human bodies. Gathering the fragments together, by the aid of a doctor, they made them out to be those of two men, three women, and a female child of ten; two male children, and a female infant. The bodies were dreadfully bruised, and stripped of every rag. In some of the native wurlies male and female garments were found, drenched with blood; also letters, newspapers, the leaves of a Bible, and part of the wrecked ship's log. Other bodies of the murdered people were discovered. The body of one woman was found in a wombat hole with a Bible, in which was a list of births, deaths, and marriages. The number killed was about twenty-six. It appears that the shipwrecked people were guided by the natives into the interior. They were induced to separate into two companies, and then killed. As the search-party followed up the tracks, they noticed that occasionally the marks of the children's feet disappeared. It was evident that the little ones became tired with their long journey, and were carried by their friends. The native women who had been captured said the white people had been divided into two parties, then some of the natives rushed upon them and held them, while others beat them upon the heads with waddies until they were dead. It was an awful outrage. This much may be said in extenuation: the blacks suffered much from lecherous whites. Like other savage tribes, they did not distinguish between the innocent and guilty, but took revenge on any who came in their way.

The search-party rounded up as many of the natives as they could, got evidence against the leaders, and hung them in the she-oak trees, over the graves of their victims. The bodies were left hanging in the trees, and the natives warned not to touch them. They remained in suspension until dissolution set in.

The ill-fated vessel that carried these unfortunate passengers was the brigantine *Maria*, bound for Van Diemen's Land.

Some of the natives were treacherous, ferocious, and revengeful, especially the great Murray tribe. No wonder that Mrs. Stephens, who had been delicately brought up in the Old Land, was sometimes afraid as she sat in her tent amongst the trees at Holdfast Bay.

In public matters connected with the young Colony, Edward Stephens took a prominent part. He became manager of the Bank of South Australia. In addition to his work as a banker he edited a weekly journal, *The Adelaide Miscellany*; but it did not pay,—he lost £400 by this literary venture. He was also a Member of Parliament, and, judging from a specimen of his oratory that the author has seen, must have been a very effective public speaker. The influence that he exerted amongst the early emigrants was evidently great. There was a saying amongst them to the effect that he had "more power than the Governor." So far as the writer has been able to ascertain, he resigned his position as manager of the Bank of South Australia in 1854, returned to England, and died a few years after. Like his brother John, his nervous system broke down. "Able and clever" is the description that an old colonist gives of him.

Edward Stephens was brother-in-law to the gifted Methodist preacher, Richard Treffry, jun., who died in Penzance in 1838. No doubt he owed much to his excellent wife, of whom the editor of the *Methodist Recorder* (20th January 1898) says: "She was the daughter of the late Mr. Baron, of Hull, whose tablet may be seen on the walls of Waltham Street Chapel. Mrs. Edward Stephens, in later life, was often seen in London Methodist circles. She and her sisters, Mrs. Richard Treffry . . . and Mrs. Edward Corderoy, were a trio of sweet saintliness, walking ever more in light and love."

PASTOR JACOB ABBOTT, ONE OF THE FOUNDERS OF THE WESLEYAN METHODIST CHURCH IN SOUTH AUSTRALIA

CHAPTER VII

HOW A METHODIST CHURCH WAS FORMED

THE early emigrants were not without the means of grace. A chaplain for the Colony (the Rev. C. B. Howard) had been appointed by King William IV. He arrived with Governor Hindmarsh in the *Buffalo*. The appointment proved to be a wise one. Mr. Howard was a man of catholic spirit. His name appears as one of the contributors to the Pioneer Methodist Chapel in Adelaide, erected in 1837.

The first Episcopalian service was held under a sail. It was borrowed by Mr. Howard from a captain in port. There were no carriers in those days, and how to get the sail transported from the seaboard to the city site was a problem. The zealous minister was equal to the solution. A hand-truck was borrowed. The Colonial Treasurer, Mr. Osmond Gilles, was pressed into service. The cleric and his lay associate dragged the sail in triumph across country, a distance of about seven miles. The first church (Trinity) was a reed-hut.

It will be a revelation to many to learn that amongst the early emigrants was David M'Laren, father of the famous preacher of Manchester. Though he did not stay long in the Colony, in more ways than one he has left his mark upon it. A beautiful little village in the hills, and a wharf at Port Adelaide, are named after him. He was sent out as General Manager of the South Australian Company; Samuel Stephens taking charge of the agricultural department.

David M'Laren was a Baptist. It will be interesting to know that he was a preacher of considerable ability. A gentleman who was in the Colony a year after its foundation, and who published his reminiscences in England, has put on record the following:—" Mr. M'Laren, the Colonial Manager of the South Australian Company, preaches on Sunday to a small but very attentive audience, and it is to be lamented that the very excellent discourses of this gentleman are not widely appreciated. A remarkable earnestness attaches to his style, and his eloquence is sometimes very forcible." He returned to England in 1841.

Thomas Quinton Stow, pioneer Congregational minister, came out in 1837. The first Congregational service was conducted in a tent. Governor Hindmarsh attended, and was accommodated with a seat on a box. The pioneer Congregational church consisted of gum-posts for uprights, and old sailcloth canvas for walls. It was thatched with reeds. Mr. Stow helped to build it with his own hands, felling timber and cutting down reeds. One of the early colonists expressed surprise that a man of Mr. Stow's talents should ever have left the Old Country. But the good man was more than satisfied. Writing to the Missionary Committee, who sent him out, he said: "What a land is this to which you have sent me! The loveliness and glory of its plains and woods, its glens and hills! But of these you will hear more from others. I cannot, however, leave it out of my estimate of God's goodness to me." He died in 1862. A fine church has been erected to his memory.

The first minister of the United Presbyterian Church was the Rev. Ralph Drummond. He came out in 1839.

But it is of the Methodist Church that we have more especially to speak. Its history is a stirring one, and is coeval with that of the Colony.

In the early history of the Methodist Church of South Australia three names will ever prominently stand out: Edward Stephens, John C. White, and Jacob Abbott.

The latter is still alive—a grand old Christian man, with clear intellect, aged eighty-five years. He lives at Glenelg (Holdfast Bay), and to him the writer is indebted for many historical facts. "Pastor Jacob Abbott" (as he has been known for many years) came by the *John Renwick*, which arrived in the early part of 1837. About sixty-five years ago he was consciously "born again" in the Wellingborough Circuit, England. His name was put on the local preachers' plan, and shortly after he left for the newly-proclaimed Colony of South Australia. For more than half a century he has been preaching the gospel. During 1897, though in his eighty-fourth year, he preached fifty-seven times, besides taking part in week-evening work and attending committee meetings of benevolent institutions. Yes, a grand old man is Jacob Abbott, as his face will show.

John C. White was born in 1813. Was accepted by the British Conference as a candidate for the ministry. His health failed, and he had to give up all thought of entering the itinerant work. Before leaving England for the new Colony of South Australia he was a local preacher in the City Road Circuit. Just before leaving London for these shores he supplied an appointment for one of the City Road ministers in the Morning Chapel. In the Methodist roll of honour for South Australia he will always occupy the foremost place. He conducted the first Methodist service on the mainland of this Colony, and until the arrival of an ordained minister, as we shall see, he was the first superintendent of a South Australian Circuit.

For more than sixty years spent in these Colonies he has been an influential worker in the Methodist Church. He now lives in New South Wales, aged eighty-six.

Edward Stephens' history (so far as it it available) we have already given. He came out in the same vessel as John C. White.

In the letter from which we have previously quoted, written by Mrs. Stephens' niece, reference is made to the service held at Holdfast Bay in Mr. Stephens' tent. By the second Sunday after his arrival (about 19th January 1837) Mr. Stephens had a large tent erected. In this Mr. John White was invited to preach. Whilst he has the honour of preaching the first Methodist sermon on the mainland, to Edward Stephens belongs the distinction of providing the first place of worship.

There is another name that South Australian Methodists must ever gratefully remember—the name of Samuel East. At this distance of time the writer has not been able to glean much respecting him. He arrived by the *Africane* on 2nd November 1836. It is more than probable that he was the first Methodist local preacher to reach these shores. With his wife, two sons, and four daughters, he landed at Nepean Bay, Kangaroo Island. Here he preached the first Methodist sermon within the boundaries of the new Colony.

Through the kindness of Samuel Stephens, the service was conducted in the South Australian Company's store.

The services at Kangaroo Island and Holdfast Bay were temporary. The settlers were merely located there till the site for the city had been fixed and the land surveyed. When this was done, as we have seen, there was a general exodus to the city site.

In Methodism there is a freemasonry of a very decided type. We fear that it is not so ardent as it once was. To a very large extent it has been called into existence and developed by our distinctive means of grace. The prayer-meeting, class-meeting, and love-feast have a tendency to create a family feeling. They give birth to spiritual affinities of a very powerful type. The world over, Methodist people feel that they are "members one of another." Heart is drawn to heart. Mutual sympathy is felt. It finds expression in the words of Charles Wesley—

> Help us to help each other, Lord,
> Each other's cross to bear;
> Let each his friendly aid afford,
> And feel his brother's care.

It was so with our pioneer Methodists in this Colony. Edward Stephens migrated from the shores of Holdfast Bay to the banks of the Torrens. A wooden house was speedily erected. It stood near the present House of Parliament. In the kitchen of this house the pioneer Methodists met for conversation and prayer. They felt that they must be doing something. The harvest of emigrants was a growing one, and the labourers were few. Open-air services were begun. They were held not far from the banks of the Torrens, near a series of huts termed "Buffalo Row." The men who conducted these services ought to be held in perpetual remembrance. They were: John C. White, from London, North; Jacob Abbott, from Wellingborough; William Pearce, from London, North; and William Croxall. In addition to these open-air services, service was also held in a small wooden hut. The little band of worshippers then moved to a more convenient room of which they had the loan. Here they were assisted by David M'Laren. On one occasion, when Mr. M'Laren came to preach, he was accompanied by His Excellency Governor Hindmarsh. The Methodist worshippers were somewhat surprised to see the preacher sit down to deliver his address.

In April 1837 the pioneer Methodists took a further step. They were without a minister, but thought they ought to form a Church. On two successive Sundays a notice was "given out" that all who desired to unite in Church fellowship, and who had tickets of removal from the Old Country, should meet in the hut of Mr. John White, on Monday evening, the 11th of May. The auspicious evening came. Fifteen persons were present: Edward Stephens, John White, Jacob Abbott, Edward Burgess, Joseph Middleton, Thomas Abbott, Isaac Jacobs, William Pearce, and William Croxall; Mesdames Stephens, White, Burgess, Pearce, Middleton, and Jacobs. These unanimously decided to form themselves into a Wesleyan Methodist Society. Two classes were formed. Brother Jacob Abbott was appointed leader of the men's class, and Brother John White was elected to take charge of the women's. The only survivors of the band who met sixty-one years ago to form a Methodist Society are Jacob Abbott and John C. White.

In more senses than one, " distance lends enchantment to the scene!" At this far-off date there is something delightfully charming about this inaugural meeting. It was the birthday of the Methodist Society in South Australia. A few emigrants had left the Old Country. They had travelled sixteen thousand miles over the mighty deep. Anchor had been cast on the shores of a practically unknown land—a land the principal occupants of which were blackfellows, dingoes, wombats, emus, and kangaroos. They were carried ashore, or waded through the water to the beach. The vessel that carried them—the last tangible link, as it were, that connected them with the Old Land—sailed away. They fixed up tents or made booths of rushes and boughs; in these they dwelt for a time by the seashore. Another migration took place. Their tents were taken down; their bough-booths were deserted; with household utensils in their hands, and with little ones toddling by their sides, they made their way through the grass and gum-trees to the site of a city that was to be. Again there was a temporary encampment. They "hutted" themselves on the banks of the Torrens, where, since creation, no white man had ever dwelt. Civilisation, so far as material surroundings are concerned, was in a state of chaos. Pork casks, packing cases, trunks, and boxes had to serve as chairs and tables. In the midst of surroundings like these, with no President of the Conference, Chairman of District, or Travelling Preacher, a small band of Methodists met together in a hut to form a Church. What vast results sometimes grow out of small beginnings! Little did these Methodist emigrants know how speedily they would realise the sentiment of one of their hymns—

> When He first the work begun,
>   Small and feeble was His day;
> Now the Word doth swiftly run,
>   Now it wins its widening way.
> More and more it spreads and grows,
>   Ever mighty to prevail;
> Sin's strongholds it now o'erthrows,
>   Shakes the trembling gates of hell.

The first class-meeting in South Australia was held on Friday evening, 15th May 1837. The leader was Jacob Abbott, and the place of meeting a hut occupied by Isaac Jacobs, on the banks of the Torrens. At this meeting Edward Stephens was present, and all the members, save John White, leader of the women's class. This class he met the following Sunday afternoon, at the house of Edward Stephens.

The pioneer band set to work in earnest. A plan was made out. The leading preachers were John White and Jacob Abbott. They did not labour in vain. The attendance at the service grew. Souls were saved and added to the Church. This was an additional inspiration.

Adelaide was now laid out, and the town lots were available. The pioneer Methodist felt the need for a more commodious place of worship. The room in which they were worshipping became too small. "And the sons of the prophets said unto Elisha, Behold, now, the place where we dwell . . . is too strait for us. Let us go, we pray thee, unto Jordan, and take thence every man a beam, and let us make a place there, where we may dwell." The monetary difficulty was evidently not so great to the "sons of the prophets" as it was to the early South Australian Methodists. However, having put their hands to the plough, they were not the men and women to turn back. They had made up their minds to build a chapel that would hold about one hundred and twenty-five persons. A piece of ground was secured in Hindley Street, near the place where the Eagle tavern now stands. A subscription list was drawn up, and Edward Stephens appointed treasurer. Not far from the site of the chapel there was an abundance of limestone. The stone was raised, and carried to the building site. The foundation was laid by Mrs. Edward Stephens. When the walls were the required height there was a delay. The carpenter who had undertaken the contract for the roof, could not get the timber. The pioneer Methodists were equal to the occasion. They stretched a tarpaulin from wall to wall. In this rough but, we think, cherished building they sang their hymns "For Believers Fighting" and "For Believers Rejoicing." Here earnest prayer was offered, and the gospel gave no uncertain sound. The first preacher to conduct service in the embryo chapel was John White. The Methodists have the credit of erecting the first stone House of God in the city. From a book published in England about 1838 by one of the early emigrants we take the following:—" There is also a Methodist chapel, built by Edward

Stephens, the manager of the South Australian Company's Bank, but, as yet, no regular minister has been appointed. Mr. M'Laren preaches in it in the morning, and it is occupied by the Methodists in the afternoon and evening."

When a small garrison is holding the fort against numerous foes, with what joy they hail the advent of reinforcements! In October 1837 such was the joy of our early Methodists. During that month three emigrant vessels arrived—the *Lady Emma*, *Katherine Stewart Forbes*, and the *Hartley*. They brought a large contingent of settlers, amongst whom were several Methodists who had credentials from the Old Country. These vessels also brought the tidings of the death of William IV. and the accession of Queen Victoria.

We can imagine with what heartiness John White and Jacob Abbott would give to the incoming Methodists the right hand of fellowship. Edward Stephens and his godly wife would not be lacking in Christian courtesy.

The first Sunday after dropping anchor, what a strange experience theirs must have been! We see them meeting in the embryo chapel on the site of a city that was yet to be built. No doubt some of them had come from the large English towns, and from the cathedral churches of Methodism. Here they saw a few buildings of a very primitive type. They were dotted about on a plain. Here and there in the city bounds were large gum-trees and numerous stumps. There were no macadamised roads or nicely-formed paths. The little chapel was in keeping with the city—roofless and windowless, with a tarpaulin stretched over the top from wall to wall. But

> Jesus, where'er Thy people meet,
> There they behold Thy mercy-seat;
> Where'er they seek Thee Thou art found,
> And every place is holy ground.

How these Methodists would sing! The "pioneer band," because their number had been increased; the "new arrivals," for the mercies of a sixteen thousand miles' voyage. Instinctively their minds would revert to the Old Land. They would think of the time—gone for ever—when in London, Manchester, Sheffield, Camborne, or Hull, they went up with the multitude to the House of God, with "the voice of joy and praise." The old pew and pulpit would rise before them, and loved faces they would never again see. We do not know what text the preacher took, but a very appropriate one would have been: "Why art thou cast down, O my soul? and why art thou disquieted within me? Hope thou in God; for I shall yet praise Him, who is the health of my countenance, and my God."

Among the Methodists who arrived in October 1837 were some local preachers: Messrs. Mincham, Lillecrapp, Sparshott, and Sleep. Later on, the *Royal Admiral* brought two more workers—Messrs. Breeze and Turner—and an accession to the membership of the infant Church.

In March 1838 the windowless apertures and tarpaulin roof were things of the past. The little chapel was finished. What a glad day that must have been! As they faced their difficulties the pioneer Methodists could say: "Who art thou, O great mountain? Before Zerubbabel thou shalt become a plain." And it was so. They brought forth the "head-stone thereof with shoutings, crying, "Grace, grace be unto it!" At the dedication service there was a "feast of fat things." John White preached in the morning from Psalm xxvi. 8: "I have loved the habitation of Thy house, and the place where Thine honour dwelleth." In the afternoon William Mincham conducted the service. His text was Haggai i. 7: "Thus saith the Lord of hosts, Consider your ways." An eloquent sermon was preached in the evening by the Rev. Thomas Q. Stow (Congregationalist). The subject was, "Redemption interesting to the Angels": and the text, 1 Pet. i. 12: "Which things the angels desire to look into."

The first printed plan was issued in 1838. No travelling preacher had yet reached the new Colony, so John White was elected Superintendent. There were two preaching places: the chapel in Hindley Street, and "Forbes' Square,"—this was a temporary settlement on the West Parklands. It lay between where the Catholic Cemetery and the Observatory now stand. A Sunday school had also been established. There were five accredited local preachers, and three brethren on trial. One of the local preachers was deputed to give special attention to the blacks. But this was not all. Said one of the pioneer Methodists: "The services had to be kept up, prior to the advent of our pastor, by persons who had to work hard for the maintenance of their households; and it was considered a bounden duty to visit the sick and poor, who, compared with the population, were not a few." How this duty was attended to, the following will show:—An elderly Methodist, with wife and family (some of whom were married), came from Cornwall. One of the married daughters was ill of consumption. A request came to Jacob Abbott that he would visit her. "I went," he says, "and when I beheld her, a feeling of sadness and awe thrilled my very being. A beautiful yet sorrowful face, giving expression to anguish of spirit, was before me. In conversation it came out that, prior to her marriage, she had known Christ, and had, with her parents, been connected with the Wesleyan Connexion. Her husband made no profession, and she soon became careless and worldly, neglecting prayer, and losing first-love. Now, death approaching, remorse and dread filled her soul. Counsel given, prayer offered, she exclaimed, amid tears—

'Oh, how could I my Saviour leave,
So soon unfaithful prove?
How could I Thy good Spirit grieve,
Or sin against Thy love?'

More prayer followed, and I left her with a gleam of hope. On visiting her again, in a day or two, I found there were some doubts lingering in her mind on account of what she called her backsliding. After assuring her that God had said, 'I will heal their backslidings; I will love them freely,' and speaking cheeringly of the wonderful love of our Heavenly Father, and of the fulness and freeness of the grace that is in Christ Jesus, she burst into tears and said, 'Now I see. Now I do believe.' Her heart was filled with peace and joy in believing. After a few days of acute suffering, borne with much patience and holy confidence, she died, triumphing in redeeming love." This is the Christlike work that the pioneer Methodists, in the absence of a pastor, did. The record is beautiful.

From the printed plan we gather that these early Methodists were true to old traditions, —they worked upon old lines. Provision was made for a love-feast and watch-night service. Not the service with which we are familiar on the last evening of the old year, but a monthly meeting, established by John Wesley. It usually began with a sermon in the evening, and continued, by singing, prayer, and exhortation, until just after midnight.

The honour of conducting the first love-feast in South Australia belongs to Jacob Abbott. It was held on 3rd June 1838. A sermon was preached from John xv. 26: "But when the Comforter is come, whom I will send unto you from the Father, even the spirit of truth, which proceedeth from the Father, He shall testify of Me." A good time followed. Among the early Methodists were a few warm-hearted members who had come from Gloucester, Cornwall, and the Isle of Wight. At this love-feast several testified, with tearful eyes and grateful hearts, of peace with God through our Lord Jesus Christ. Soon after, a glorious revival took place.

The names of the South Australian pioneer Methodists, and the work they did for God and the Methodist Church, deserve to be put on perpetual record. With others, they had come to colonise a knew and unknown land. The circumstances in which they were placed were peculiar, —it was a transition indeed. They might have been so absorbed in the material as to lose sight of the spiritual. An Episcopal and Congregational minister had reached the new land. These had formed Churches. The pioneer Methodists might have thrown in their lot with them. But no: "If I forget thee, O Jerusalem, let my right hand forget her cunning." In the absence of ordained minister, quarterly meeting, district meeting, or Conference, they began to preach, formed a society, built a chapel, established a Sunday school, made out a plan, visited the sick, and deputed one of their number to give special attention to the blacks. But they sadly needed—as Jacob Abbott said sixty years later—"a pastor to lead and to guide." They applied directly and indirectly to the Missionary Committee, but no answer came. The Society was now in troubled waters. John White desired to be relieved of his responsibility. What could the members of the little Church do? They made their position a matter of earnest prayer. How that prayer was answered we must reserve for the next chapter.

REV. WILLIAM LONGBOTTOM, FIRST WESLEYAN MISSIONARY TO SOUTH AUSTRALIA

CHAPTER VIII

THE TRAVELLING PREACHER AND HOW HE CAME

AT the close of the last century there was a Methodist class leader living near Bingley, in the West Riding of Yorkshire. His name was Thomas Longbottom. To this worthy man and his wife, in 1799, a son was born. They named him William. That son was to travel far and wide, and to do important work in connection with Methodism. From his infancy he was taught the fear of the Lord.

To Methodists living in a Conference town and its vicinity the gathering of the preachers was always an event of great importance. It was then that they had an opportunity of hearing the leading men of Methodism. The Conference of 1818 was held at Leeds. Joseph Benson was appointed to preach. Of him it is said that, in spite of a weak, shrill voice, the effect of his preaching was overwhelming. "His weeping and trembling congregations were apt to think of him ... as an Elijah, surrounded by invisible hosts. At the close of his sermons there would be a strain of appeal so cogent, and inspired from above, that every word was like an arrow of the Almighty."

Thomas Longbottom travelled to Leeds to hear Joseph Benson, taking with him his son William. It was a memorable journey. The word came with power to William's heart, and he earnestly sought salvation.

About this time there was a spiritual awakening at Bingley. A special unction attended the ministry of James Blackett and Joseph Beaumont. William Longbottom began to meet in class. Here he became associated with Thomas Cryer, who married the saintly Mary Burton, with the memoir of whom Methodists were once well familiar. There is no record of any special time when peace came to his soul. He took an active part in Sunday-school work and in the Friday evening prayer-meeting. In this meeting three generations of his family were represented—Matthew, Thomas, and William Longbottom : grandfather, father, and son. Frequently their prayers followed in succession.

In 1824 William removed to Wakefield. Here he was placed on the plan as a local preacher. Next year he was recommended as a candidate for mission work. While at Wakefield, it was his privilege to be associated with two noted Methodist preachers: William Atherton and James Dixon.

In 1826 he was advised by the Missionary Committee to hold himself in readiness to go to Van Diemen's Land. The summons to leave was forwarded, but, through some miscarriage, he did not receive it. Another preacher took his place, and the letter was returned to the Mission House. He was then sent by John Stephens, President of the Conference, to supply in the Otley Circuit, and a few months afterwards was appointed to Newcastle-under-Lyne.

The Missionary Committee decided that he should labour in Madras. In 1828 he was stationed at Reading, so that he might take lessons from Thomas H. Squance, in the Tamil language. At the ensuing Conference he married Miss England, of Bingley, and shortly after left England, in company with Thomas Cryer and other missionaries, for Madras.

As they sailed away from their native land, little conception did William Longbottom and his young wife have of the varied experiences through which they were to pass, or of the important work they were to do in a Colony not yet constituted.

In the list of stations for 1831-32 we read: "Negapatam—William Longbottom." Next year he was stationed at Madras Second; the year following, Negapatam and Melnattam. His last station was Madras. In the list of stations for 1836-37 there is a great change. Now we read: "Cape District.—Capetown and Somerset—William Longbottom." The explanation is (as every Indian missionary will surmise), failure in health. He entered into his work, shall we say, with such indiscreet zeal that his constitution was undermined, and the foundation of a chronic and lifelong malady was laid.

A short residence at the Cape made a temporary

improvement in his health. But his heart was in India, and to that field he returned. Meanwhile the Missionary Committee, in consideration of his health, had appointed him to Swan River, a convict settlement on the western coast of Australia.

Himself, wife, and child set sail from India *viâ* Mauritius. In one sense the voyage was a disastrous one. The missionary and family were ultimately landed in a Colony that, as yet, had no place on the Minutes of Conference. They were detained at Mauritius nine weeks. From Mauritius they reached Van Diemen's Land. This was the Colony to which he had been appointed in 1826, an appointment that was not then effected through the miscarriage of a letter. At Van Diemen's Land they had to remain five months, awaiting an opportunity to reach Swan River.

On the 9th of June 1838 the *Fanny*, a small vessel of thirty-five tons, set sail for King George's Sound. By this vessel Mr. Longbottom, with his wife and child, had taken passage. Along the Australian coast terrific weather is sometimes experienced. It was so on this occasion. The vessel had not cleared Van Diemen's Land before rough weather set in. Twice she put back for shelter. For a time fine weather was experienced. On Sunday, the 17th of June, the wind blew a perfect hurricane. On the following Thursday the water changed colour, and soundings were taken. The captain, not being able to take observations for several days, and not knowing how near the vessel had drifted to land, thought she was passing over a sandbar. It was now about nine o'clock at night. Having had no rest for several nights, Mr. Longbottom and wife tried to get a little sleep. About half-past one in the morning the sea broke on board in all directions. The captain found himself in only seven fathoms of water. All attempts to sail were fruitless. The vessel struck. "About one," Mrs. Longbottom says, "I was aroused by an unusual rolling of the vessel. Instantly I told my husband that I was sure we were in the surf. After a moment he was convinced that my fears were too well grounded, and, throwing on his rough jacket, was in the act of reaching his cap to go on deck when the vessel struck. No time was to be lost. Providentially, we had lain down in our clothes. I hurried on little William's shoes and cap, and, after commending ourselves to God, we endeavoured to get on deck. We found the hatches down, and it was some time before we could make those on deck hear. When we did get out, an awful scene was before us." At times the party were up to their waists in water. The captain ascended the rigging, and in the distance saw a low, dark ridge. It was land. Mrs. Longbottom proceeds: "The sailors cut away the boat; but it drifted away the moment it was lowered. The captain had swum ashore with a rope. He lost his hold, and was unable to return. At length a sailor succeeded in reaching shore with a rope, which he made fast, and then returned to render assistance to us. We put our dear boy over the side of the vessel first; the men handed him to the captain, who carried him through the surf. You may form some idea of what our feelings were when we knew that our only child was safe. It was now my turn, but I had not the courage to jump overboard when the surf receded, and Mr. Longbottom was obliged to push me off. I lost my hold of the rope, and was several minutes under water. My dear William, seeing my situation, instantly plunged in after me, and laid hold of my dress. We were mercifully preserved, and all got safely through that dreadful surf; but I was extremely exhausted, and unable to stand when I reached the beach. All went behind a sandbank and lay down among the bushes to await the morning light. We were dreadfully cold, being in our wet clothes, and unable to make a fire." The cold must have been intense. In addition to wet clothes it was winter-time, and one of the coldest months of the year.

The day after the shipwreck a party of blacks came upon the scene. It must have been with mingled feelings that the shipwrecked people saw them approach. What were their intentions? Friendly or hostile? Did their advent mean life or death? Their fears were soon set at rest. The natives brought a firestick, created a fire, and pointed out their water holes.

Strange to relate, the same tribe of natives that showed such kindness to this shipwrecked party was the tribe who, two years afterwards, brutally murdered the crew and passengers of the ill-fated *Maria*. The *Maria* was on her way to the same port from which the *Fanny* had set sail. The murders took place not far from the spot where Mr. and Mrs. Longbottom were wrecked. About seven weeks the party were at the mercy of the blacks. The captain says: "They were well disposed, and the most inoffensive race that he had ever met."

The day after the visit of the natives (being Sunday), a little service was held, in which the shipwrecked people gave thanks to God for preservation from a watery grave.

The captain decided that the better plan would be to attempt to find a way to some station overland. Mrs. Longbottom says: "We had no alternative but either to accompany the ship's party or be left behind in the bush. Accordingly, Mr. Longbottom prepared for our departure by packing up a pair of blankets, a few biscuits, and a little wine and water; the whole of which he fastened on his back, and we set out, 'not knowing whither we went.' But sleeping on the damp ground, together with struggling so long in the surf, had made me so stiff, and had brought on such rheumatism, that I could scarcely walk at all. I dragged on about five miles, when I could go no farther. I felt our situation peculiarly trying at this time; the temper of our captain was very odd, and the whole party was likely to be detained on my account. After resting for a few hours, Mr. Longbottom proposed that we should all return to the tent, and endeavour to gain fuller knowledge of our situation, and prepare ourselves better for travelling. I believe that it was the Spirit of God that dictated this proposal, for all agreed to it and immediately prepared to return. I walked back in much pain, and about midnight we arrived at the tent, and found everything just as we left it."

A quantity of provisions had been obtained from the wreck, and the dingy had drifted ashore. Captain Gill then set to work to lengthen and repair it. About half a mile inland the shipwrecked party discovered a lagoon. It appeared to run parallel with the beach. It was what is now known as the Coorong, connected with the river Murray. On this sheet of water Captain Gill hoped to set sail.

One day, as the captain and men were labouring at the dingy, they met with a strange surprise. A few white men were seen coming down the coast in the direction of the wreck. They proved to be companions in misfortune. Another vessel (the *Elizabeth*) had been wrecked about fifty miles eastward. The leg-weary travellers were the shipwrecked captain and his crew. Although met together under unfortunate circumstances, it was, "Hail, fellow! Well met!" Captain Tindall, of the *Elizabeth*, had with him both chart and compass. This was a great comfort, as Mr. and Mrs. Longbottom and party now knew in what direction to seek help. The two captains laboured together. The dingy was finished. It was too small to carry the whole party. The captains decided to leave the missionary, wife, child, and three sailors in the bush, whilst they and some of the sailors made for Encounter Bay. At this place there was a whaling station, and here they hoped to get a larger boat, in which to tranship the whole party. They set sail on the Coorong. Steering westward, they reached the mouth of the Murray, not far distant from the fishery at Encounter Bay.

In the letter describing their experiences Mrs. Longbottom says: "During the absence of the party was a truly anxious time. We felt that, should any disaster befall them, or the boat, so that we could not return, we had no human means left of ever getting away. However, in less than a week, two of the men returned with the joyful intelligence that they had been to Encounter Bay, and that the captain would be up in two days with a large whaleboat for us. We waited several days after the time appointed, but, seeing no captain or boat, we started in the little boat, taking with us our blankets, a change of linen for each of us, and a small case with a few of my husband's most valuable papers, with a supply of provisions. We left the bush on the 7th of August, having spent forty-five days from the time of our wreck in a state of great anxiety and suspense. It was a beautiful day when we started. The men rowed; Mr. Longbottom steered; and I baled out the water. Being a fine moonlight night, we kept on till midnight, when we hauled up, but could not land. We were obliged to sit in the boat all night. It was dreadfully cold, and a very heavy dew; but mercifully we took no cold, though without any shelter, and the boat very leaky. At daybreak we set off again, and about ten o'clock met the captain with a large boat. We changed boats, and about one o'clock crossed the Murray River. Here we landed, and stayed until sunset, when we again set sail in the boat."

Eventually the party reached Encounter Bay. Here they were kindly entertained by Captain Wright and his good lady. The whole trip was indeed providential. To reach Encounter Bay they had to cross the mouth of the Murray. This was attended by risk. It was in an attempt to negotiate the mouth of the Murray that Sir John Jeffcott and Captain Blinkinsopp lost their lives. Sir John Jeffcott was the first judge of the new Colony. In opposition to Colonel Light, he thought that the city should be at Encounter Bay. To prove that the mouth of the Murray was navigable, in company with Captain Blinkinsopp and others he tried to sail out of it. The boat was wrecked, and only two of the party, after a desperate struggle, escaped with their lives. This was not many months before Captain Gill, with his precious cargo, crossed it. "We did not ship," said he, "a spoonful of water."

Captain Tindall travelled overland from Encounter Bay to Adelaide, carrying with him tidings of the wreck of the *Elizabeth* and the *Fanny*.

What a flutter there must have been amongst the little band of pioneer Methodists! One of the shipwrecked people was a Methodist preacher! Was his advent an answer to prayer? Would they be able to secure his services? How could negotiations be opened up? Already their hearts went out in sympathy towards him. A wife and little child made the position more pathetic. Through Edward Stephens, communication was at once made to the shipwrecked minister. He requested them to come to Adelaide, offered them a home and every assistance in his power.

A vessel, the *Lady Wellington*, was on her way from Sydney to Adelaide. The passage had been a stormy one. She called at various ports for refuge; amongst others, Encounter Bay. This was a fitting opportunity for Mr. Longbottom, his wife and child, to reach Adelaide. Again there was a reverse. As the vessel tried to cross the outer bar, at the entrance to Port Adelaide, she ran aground. Here the passengers and cargo had to be discharged. But kind friends were at hand. Edward Stephens arranged for a boat to bring the Methodist preacher and his family up the port river. A conveyance was then provided in which they could travel to Adelaide.

What a strange and bitter experience! As we read it we seem to hear the shriek of the wind, the fall of the rain, and the roar of the breakers. Detained nine weeks at Mauritius; five months at Van Diemen's Land; wrecked on the South Australian coast; escaping through the surf by means of a rope; spending about seven weeks in the Australian bush—this in the depth of winter, at the mercy of black savages; sailing down the Coorong in a leaky boat—the missionary's wife baling out the water; sitting all night in the boat on the Coorong, wet and half frozen; crossing the mouth of the Murray; setting sail in another vessel for Port Adelaide; finally running aground at the entrance to the port river. Verily, in the service of God the Apostle Paul had no monopoly of vivid and strange experiences. Little did the young missionary and his wife, who set sail from Old England in 1829, know of the strange vicissitudes that lay before them.

"Weeping may endure for a night, but joy cometh in the morning." The storm ceased. The waves subsided. The dark clouds were dissipated. Soon the missionary and his wife and child[1] were safely anchored in the little wooden residence of Edward Stephens. Here they received a warm English welcome.

In a temporal sense the shipwrecked missionary had lost his all. The library and papers could not be replaced, but kind friends came to their rescue, and all their material wants were supplied.

Is it matter for surprise that the Methodist pioneers looked upon Mr. Longbottom's advent as a godsend? Said one of them, some time after: "We could not get on, for we could not agree who should be superintendent; but God pitied us, and sent us a minister by wrecking one on our coasts."

The Colony had not been founded three years. It had no place on the Minutes of Conference, but Mr. Longbottom found a Methodist chapel erected; a Sunday school formed; several local preachers; a printed plan; and a society consisting of about

---

[1] The son is with us to-day. One of the leading merchants of our city.

sixty members. Verily, to-day we owe a debt of gratitude to Edward Stephens, John C. White, Jacob Abbott, and the other local preachers whose names stand on the first printed plan.

There came another eventful day in the experience of the early Methodists. It was when the shipwrecked minister stood up in their little limestone chapel and preached the gospel. His text was 2 Peter iii. 18: "Grow in grace." As he talked to them about the necessity and importance of practical piety, the tears of gratitude fell from many eyes, and hearts were made glad. The desire of their souls had been fulfilled. The end they had long tried to compass had now been attained. The Episcopalians and Congregationalists had their pastor, and so had the Methodists. "Well do I remember," says Jacob Abbott, "him presiding at our first love-feast after his arrival. The tears ran down his cheeks while he exclaimed: 'I was hungry, and ye gave me meat; thirsty, and ye gave me drink; naked, and ye clothed me'"; and how devoutly he thanked the Lord for having spared him, and allowed him again to blow the gospel trumpet in the land of the living."

But Mr. Longbottom's station was Swan River. Could he remain in South Australia? The claims and persuasions of the friends were urgent. There was no immediate means for reaching Swan River. In Adelaide he had to remain, awaiting instructions. Meanwhile the Society was busy. They were not going to let so favourable an opportunity slip. Negotiations were opened up with the Rev. Joseph Orton, Chairman of the Van Diemen's Land District. A memorial from the Adelaide trustees was sent to the Missionary Committee in London. It may be seen in the *Methodist Magazine* for 1839. The memorialists say: "On Mr. Longbottom's arrival amongst us we were enabled to introduce those parts of the regular discipline which had not been previously brought into operation; and the results are already cheering and satisfactory; and we feel quite confident that if he be permitted to remain with us, we shall be fully competent to meet the expenses required for the maintenance of himself and family, without troubling the Committee at all on the subject of funds. Since his arrival we have enjoyed much prosperity and peace; we have raised £500 for a new chapel; our Society is increased and our prospects brightened; and we hope that the unanimous appeal of the stewards, leaders, local preachers, and trustees of the Methodist Society in South Australia will meet with that kind attention which we think the circumstances of our case require." The appeal was granted. Who could resist so eloquent and graceful a plea? In the English Minutes of Conference for 1839 a fresh line appears: "Adelaide, South Australia—William Longbottom."

For a time Mr. and Mrs. Longbottom resided under the roof of Edward Stephens. Finally a cottage was rented in Grenfell Street. The settlement was still in a very rude state. Many of the houses were of a temporary character, and rents were high. The Methodist missionary and his wife had to content themselves with two small rooms and a smaller kitchen. There was no ceiling. The building did not keep out heat in summer nor rain in winter. For this indifferent shelter they had to pay £50 per year.

Before concluding this chapter we notice a very singular circumstance. Before his appointment to India in 1829, William Longbottom was sent, one

Sunday morning, by the Missionary Committee to preach at City Road Chapel. He arrived early. Several questions were put to the caretaker as to the order of the service. The worthy man's suspicions were aroused. "Why do you wish to know?" he asked. Said the youthful preacher: "I am to preach here this morning." "You going to preach?" was the rejoinder; "it is a downright shame to send such raw-boned fellows to preach here. I tell you, the congregation will be terribly disappointed." Amongst the early emigrants was this caretaker, his wife and family. They formed a part of the pioneer Methodist band. Imagine the good man's surprise when the shipwrecked missionary proved to be the young man whom he had so discouraged a few years before at City Road Chapel.

CLARENDON: PART OF A SOUTH AUSTRALIAN COUNTRY CIRCUIT

CHAPTER IX

HOW THE CHURCH GREW

UNTIL the arrival of a preacher appointed by the British Conference, there was something lacking in the constitution of the pioneer Church. With the romantic arrival of Mr. Longbottom that want was supplied. Jacob Abbott describes his preaching as "fervent, animated, winning." Souls were converted. The chapel was filled. It became too small. The Church was not only in a healthy condition, but was fast growing. The General Superintendent of Australian Missions (John Waterhouse) was delighted. Writing to the Missionary Secretaries in London, in 1839, he says: "From Adelaide the report of the work is most cheering. I have seen a letter from Mrs. Longbottom to a friend which has greatly delighted me."

The memorial addressed to the Missionary Committee, quoted in our last chapter, speaks of "much prosperity and peace," "bright prospects," an "increase in membership." There is also a very suggestive line: "We have raised £500 for a new chapel." At this time Mr. Longbottom had only been in Adelaide a little more than two months.

A new chapel had become imperative. In addition to a contribution of £55, Edward Stephens gave a piece of land for a site in Gawler Place. On 27th November 1838 Governor Gawler laid the foundation-stone. It would seat five hundred persons, and cost about £2000. At the opening services, early in 1839, Mr. Longbottom preached in the morning from Luke xxiv. 46: "Thus it is written, and thus it behoved Christ to suffer, and to rise from the dead the third day." In the afternoon an address was given to the children. The evening service was conducted by the Rev. Thomas Q. Stow (Congregationalist).

The joy of the early Methodists in the erection of this large and beautiful chapel must have been tinged with sadness. Could they forget the little pioneer building in Hindley Street? Would not the windowless walls and tarpaulin roof rise before them? Would they not remember the pew in which they sat, and the pulpit in which Mr. Longbottom first stood before them? Yes; there were associations connected with the firstborn of their zeal and love that could never be forgotten. If the opening of the new chapel in Gawler Place was like a resurrection, the closing service in the old must have been something like a burial. If the one meant the realisation of greater possibilities in a grander tabernacle, the other meant "putting off" the old body that had been so serviceable. However, we may well leave the clay tabernacle to enter a house not made with hands, eternal in the heavens. So our pioneer Methodists could well afford to leave their little building, with its dear associations, to enter a larger and more perfect structure, in which they would do a nobler work for God. So long as change means progress, all is well. To the early South Australian Methodists such was its meaning.

New preaching places were taken up. The first service at North Adelaide was conducted by Mr. Longbottom in a hut near Pennington Terrace.

Suburban openings followed, and new classes were formed. Jacob Abbott's class was divided into two—the minister taking one, and William Collins the other; whilst the old leader formed a new class at North Adelaide.

In October 1839 there came another gala day in the history of the pioneer Methodist Church: this was the centenary of Wesleyan Methodism.

. . . . .

During the reign of the second George the moral decline in England reached its lowest ebb. Drunkenness, profanity, sensuality, and infidelity abounded. The Puritan revival was spent. Its collapse proved how impossible it is to make a nation righteous by Act of Parliament. Methodism had not yet come into existence. Everywhere there was licentiousness and extravagance. It seemed as though the Sun of Righteousness in England had set, and the nation was sitting in darkness and the shadow of death. But brighter and better times were dawning. The Sun of Righteousness was to arise with healing in his wings. It was indeed a "crooked and perverse generation"; but in the providence of God a band of men were raised up who were to "shine as lights in the world," holding forth to others the Word of life. At the head of these men were John and Charles Wesley. At the same time the Spirit of God moved upon the hearts of the people. In the latter part of 1739 several persons, who felt the burden of sin, came to John Wesley in London for guidance and instruction. They asked him to spend some time with them in prayer, and to advise them how to flee from the wrath to come. He arranged to meet them every Thursday evening. The number grew. This was the origin of the Methodist Society—a Society that was to exert a powerful influence for good, not only in Great Britain, but throughout the world.

The centenary of the birth of this Society fell in October 1839. It was right that the British Conference should make it an occasion for special thanksgiving to God. The Conference of 1838 recommended the "members and friends of the Wesleyan Methodist Societies throughout the Connexion to unite in grateful and devout acknowledgment of the great and numerous blessings involved in the commencement and progress of Methodism by holding simultaneous religious meetings on Friday, October 25th, 1839."

The Society in South Australia was not yet three years old, but it was loyal to the recommendation of the British Conference. It did not stay to inquire, " By whom shall Jacob arise, for he is small ? " Whilst the Methodists in the Old Land were rejoicing together, and giving their thousands, the pioneer Methodists in the youngest British offshoot were not wanting in charity or zeal. On Friday, 25th October 1839, meetings were held in the newly-erected chapel in Gawler Place. In the afternoon the foundation-stone of a chapel to be erected in North Adelaide was laid by Mrs. Edward Stephens. Over £600 was raised. This was devoted to the extension of Methodism in the new Colony.

Mr. Longbottom's constitution had been undermined in India. Shipwreck, exposure in the bush for several weeks, discomforts incidental to a new settlement, and hard work in connection with the establishment of Methodism in South Australia, enfeebled him. One Sunday evening, preaching on " the great white throne," suddenly he had to stop and sit down. Edward Stephens and Dr. Lichfield (who was in the congregation) went to his assistance. The service came to an abrupt termination. The congregation were alarmed, but were somewhat comforted when Dr. Lichfield told them that there was no immediate danger. It was weakness of the heart. The mental and physical strain in connection with the mission was too much, and the climate was trying: to the great grief of the people, the pioneer preacher who had been so mysteriously cast upon their shores, had to seek a removal. He was transferred to Tasmania.

. . . . .

On 4th September 1838 an important meeting was held at City Road Chapel. The President of the Conference (Thomas Jackson) was in the chair. John Hannah, Robert Alder, Edmund Grindrod, Jabez Bunting, Richard Treffry, sen., John Beecham, and Elijah Hoole were present. Long before the time appointed for the meeting the chapel was crowded. It was an ordination and valedictory service. Peter Jones (the Indian chief) was about to return to his native land. John Waterhouse, an esteemed minister, who had travelled twenty-nine years at home, was about to sail to Van Diemen's Land. He had been appointed Superintendent of Wesleyan Missions in Australia and Polynesia. No doubt, in his official capacity, he had been on the lookout for men of special promise. Two or three of such were about to set sail with him. There was the gifted and devoted John H. Bumby. There was also Samuel Ironside, whose long and laborious life spent in Colonial work deserves more than a passing record. Seated next to John H. Bumby was a young brother who was to make his mark in Australian missionary work. It was John Eggleston—a name that will long be remembered and revered in this part of the world. At the call of Thomas Jackson this young missionary came forward to give "an account of his conversion and call to the ministry." Said he: "Until the Conference, I had no idea of leaving my native land. There Mr. Waterhouse pressingly requested me to accompany him to Hobart Town. I felt such a consciousness of the presence of God, and that in His presence I could be happy in any part of the world, that I did not see any strong objections. I knew that I had a mother who loved me dearly, and that even my leaving her to go into the ministry at home had cost her many a pang. I wrote to her, however, and I received an answer of assent, which overwhelmed me. I saw clearly the finger of God in this dispensation, and that a blight would be brought on my ministerial character if I resisted this call. I therefore yielded to the impression; and I present myself before you this evening, feeling more than I have ever felt of the missionary spirit, entreating an interest in your prayers, and trusting that the blessing of Heaven will continually rest upon you."

A few days after this meeting, Messrs. Waterhouse, Bumby, Ironside, Eggleston, with two other missionaries, went down to Gravesend, accompanied by Jabez Bunting and two of the Missionary Secretaries, and set sail for the Foreign Mission Field.

John Eggleston's appointment was to Van Diemen's Land. In 1840 he was transferred to Adelaide to take the place vacated by Mr. Longbottom. Writing to the Missionary Committee, he says: "I arrived at this place last Sabbath morning. We had a stormy, uncomfortable passage of seventeen days from Hobart Town. The vessel in which we came has not been able to reach the port, in consequence of the wind being unfavourable for coming up the creek. We anchored on the outside of the bar, a distance of thirty miles from the port, on Saturday evening. The captain, knowing that I was anxious to be in Adelaide on the Sabbath, kindly offered to send his boat the next morning to the pilot's station, which was abreast of us, six or eight miles off; from thence we were to walk through the bush two miles, procure a boat to convey us across the creek to the port, and then proceed by land to the city, which is six miles in the interior. I thankfully embraced the opportunity; left Mrs. Eggleston and child to come up in the vessel; and arrived in the chapel a little before twelve o'clock. The local preacher who was officiating recognised me, and beckoned me into the pulpit. I introduced myself to the congregation, and concluded the service. In the evening we had the chapel nearly full, and I felt myself much comforted while preaching."

John Eggleston was well received by the people. Said one of the early Methodists: " We found that we had one in our midst who, though young, was strong—so renewed our efforts in the work of the Lord, regretting, at the same time, the removal of our first beloved and devoted pastor."

The characteristic zeal of the young preacher comes out in his anxious endeavour to reach his appointment. It was Saturday evening when the vessel dropped anchor off what is now known as the Semaphore. Nothing could be done till Sunday morning. Leaving his wife and child on board, he was rowed to the beach. A walk of two miles through the bush (now a popular watering-place) brought him to Port Adelaide. A journey of seven miles was then before him. Weary and travel-stained, he reached the Gawler Place Chapel. John White was conducting the service. Soon the young missionary was by his side in the pulpit. Looking round the church for a moment, taking in his new surroundings, he offered prayer, and then announced his text (1 Cor. xiv. 1): "Follow after Charity."

When John Eggleston arrived, the Colony had only been founded a little more than four years. Adelaide was still in an embryo condition. The young missionary had his domestic difficulties and discouragements. To the Committee in London he writes: "I am perplexed to know how to act with regard to the rental and furnishing of a house. . . . The cottage Mr. Longbottom has occupied has two small rooms and a smaller kitchen, all open to the roof (without ceiling), and it affords very little shelter, especially from the heat; and yet it is a favour to have this at £50 a year. The rents are fearfully high, furniture of all kinds is excessively dear."

No doubt the Missionary Committee would be sympathetic, but we do not think it could do much, in a practical way, to help the young preacher in his domestic trials. How he finally settled down we are not in a position to say. It is more than probable that he had to put into practice the teaching of Scripture: "Be content with such things as ye have."

John Eggleston, like other young pioneer preachers, apart from domestic discomforts, had some peculiar experiences. The orthodox custom, in the early days, was for a rider to wear spurs. In fact it has been said that in those unconventional times, if a man wore a pair of trousers and spurs he was well dressed. So far as the wearing of the spurs is concerned, the young Methodist missionary conformed to custom—with what effect we shall see. One of the "preaching places" was at Willunga, thirty miles from Adelaide. A horse had been purchased for the use of the preacher. . . . The rider put on his spurs, took his seat in the saddle, and started for Willunga. Riding down one of the main streets of the city, he was accosted by a friend. Leaning over the saddle, for a little conversation, one of the spurs got into action. Unaccustomed to such treatment, especially from a Methodist preacher, in a most determined manner the steed rebelled. It began to caper. To fall off in one of the leading streets of the city (Rundle Street) would indeed be humiliating. No doubt each leg of the rider would grip the horse firmly. In this way both spurs got into action. The consequence was, that very soon there was a divorce between the steed and its rider. John Eggleston found himself prostrate in Rundle Street, with bruised face and sprained ankle, whilst the liberated steed quietly made its way back to the stable. The congregation at Willunga were disappointed. We get wisdom by experience, sometimes of a very painful character. No doubt in every way the steed reaped the advantage. He had one journey the less, and next time the rider mounted him we expect the spurs would be left behind.

Mr. Eggleston's stay in the Colony was not long. He returned to Tasmania, travelled subsequently in Victoria and New South Wales, occupied some of the highest positions that the Connexion could give, and died in 1879, aged sixty-six years.

In the infant Colony of South Australia he did a good work. Under his ministry many souls were convinced of sin, and converted to God. Often he would be at Jacob Abbott's house, in North Adelaide, by daybreak, tapping at the window or door. "Come on, brother!" he would exclaim. In a few minutes the two would be on their knees, pouring out their souls before God for the salvation of sinners, and the fulness of blessing upon the Church. In an unmistakable way prayer was answered. There were "showers of blessings." Says one of the Methodist pioneers : " Great numbers were brought to God, and believers experienced a deeper measure of divine grace." The "Church quickly extended her borders, and rapidly increased in numbers through conversions, and accessions from England." There were now nearly three hundred members in Society, four chapels, and about twenty-one other preaching places.

It was during Mr. Eggleston's time that Jacob Abbott was called upon to give up his secular employment, and work as a lay assistant in connection with the Methodist Church. He was the first Methodist Home Missionary in South Australia. His appointment came about in this way. Amongst the Methodist pioneers was a man who has immortalised himself. His name stands in the same category as that of Richard Arkwright and James Watt. To John Ridley, Methodist miller and local preacher, belongs the honour of inventing the reaping and threshing machine. This was about seven years after the Colony was founded. It has revolutionised agriculture, and reduced the cost of production to a minimum. The machine strips the heads of wheat from the stalk, and threshes them, whilst the horses are drawing it to and fro in the field. It can only be used in a dry climate, where the head will easily break off.

Jacob Abbott was keeping a store at North Adelaide. One day the Methodist miller called upon him. The following dialogue took place:— Said the Methodist storekeeper to the Methodist miller: "You seem busy carting flour into Adelaide. I have a horse and dray doing very little just now. Could I assist in any way?" "What would you wish for the use of them?" was the response. Said Jacob Abbott: "About thirty shillings a week; you to find horse-feed and driver." "Agreed," said the Methodist miller; "but I would rather pay you that to go about the country to preach and visit the people, and render help to our minister." Jacob Abbott was taken by surprise—a very agreeable one. The matter was laid before the overwrought John Eggleston: he hailed the proposal with joy. For nearly two years this arrangement was continued, the Methodist miller, John Ridley, meeting all expense.

Jacob Abbott had some amusing experiences.

In turn he had to conduct service at Willunga. During one of his visits the brother who usually entertained him was not able to do so, but he had very kindly made arrangements for the preacher elsewhere. He was to stay with an old Scotch couple. The welcome was a very hearty one. After the preacher was seated, the good wife came in with a pan half-full of warm water. He was asked to take a seat on the sofa. The pan of water was placed in front of him. "Now, sir," said the old lady, "let me take off your butes." Jacob Abbott was quite disconcerted. He must have felt as abashed as Peter. There was the same indignant remonstrance. "Oh dear, no," said he; "what do you wish to do?" The reply was: "Ye dinna ken we Scotch Methodees do always obey the Lord's bidding to wash the saint's feet, and it's vary refreeshing; and ye'll get a cup o' tea after it." Jacob Abbott looked inquiringly at the husband. He nodded assent; and the washing took place. After well drying with a clean, white towel, the old lady said: "Now, we'll take tea, and ye'll be right for your Master's work to-morrow."

Other early emigrants showed their regard for the Methodist Home Missionary in a less self-humiliating way. At the Meadows, about thirty-four miles from Adelaide, two gentlemen (Messrs. Stanford and Burley) had established a dairy farm and cattle run. As soon as the Methodist missionary came, himself and horse were well provided for, and a stock-boy was told to mount a horse and inform the surrounding settlers of his arrival. At M'Laren Vale he was well cared for by Mr. and Mrs. Colton, parents of Sir John Colton, of whom we shall have to speak. They were engaged in sheep and dairy farming, and the son, who rose to distinction in the new Colony, tended his father's sheep.

Some of the pioneer services were held under peculiar circumstances. At one " preaching place," a few miles from Adelaide, some gum-planks served as seats, a flour cask for a pulpit, and a small pannikin suspended from the roof, and furnished with oil and wick, gave light to preacher and people. Materially it may have been a " dim religious light," not so the illuminating power of the Holy Spirit. At a place called Mount Barker

REV. JOHN EGGLESTON, SECOND WESLEYAN METHODIST MISSIONARY TO SOUTH AUSTRALIA (now the site of a fine town), a few miles from Adelaide, service was held in a blacksmith's shop. The anvil did duty as pulpit, and the hubs of dray wheels, with planks laid thereon, served as seats. If the blacksmith's anvil, during the week, gave "no uncertain sound," we are sure that the same might be said of the Word of God as proclaimed from the anvil on the Sunday.

John Eggleston was succeeded by John Weatherstone.

Writing to the Missionary Committee in London, in 1840, Mr. Eggleston said: "The state of the Aborigines here is most deplorable. I passed by a tribe as I came from the port to the city. The children were running about in a state of nudity, and the adults had a kind of blanket thrown carelessly around them. They are friendly, and spend the day in strolling about the town, begging provisions. From what I have heard, there is much prospect of success, could missionaries be sent out to labour amongst them." Mr. Weatherstone took a great interest in the blacks. He collected about nine hundred and fifty of the words spoken by the Murray River tribe, with their equivalents in English. It was his earnest desire and prayer that the Missionary Committee would relieve him from English work, and allow him to go as a missionary to the Aborigines. The request was not granted. It may have been well for both Mr. Weatherstone and the Aborigines if his desire had been fulfilled. Evidently, he was an enthusiastic in missionary work amongst the South Australian blacks, and had a genius for it. Mr. Weatherstone was a minister of ability, but his stay in the Colony was not a happy one. There were financial reverses, as we have pointed out, in the young Colony, and there were spiritual reverses in the Methodist Church. Perhaps, to a certain extent, one was the reflex of the other. The Church (still in its infancy) had to pass through a time of trial and trouble. There was a secession, in which, unfortunately, Jacob Abbott took part. The seceders formed a new organisation, termed "The Australian Methodist Society." It was not long-lived. Jacob Abbott became pastor of a Christian Disciple Church, and continued in that capacity until obliged to resign through weight of years. Ultimately, Mr. Weatherstone was recalled to England, became Superintendent of Missions in Sierra Leone, and finally resigned his position as a Methodist preacher.

After an absence of about four years, Mr. Longbottom returned to Adelaide. His second advent was hailed with joy, but his life's work was drawing to a close. In the Minutes of the British Conference for 1846 the following occurs: —" Adelaide—Jonathan Innes. William Longbottom returning home for recovery of his health." The trip to England was not taken. Gradually he became weaker, and on the 29th of July 1849 he finished his course with joy. To his wife he often said: "The great Atonement was made for me. I have an interest in the great sacrifice, and in the living Mediator. I have no fear of death; all will be right at last." One morning he said: "That verse has been on my mind all night: indeed it is always with me—

> 'Tis love! 'tis love! Thou diedst for me,
>   I hear Thy whisper in my heart.
> The morning breaks! The shadows flee!
>   Pure universal love Thou art.
> To me, to all, Thy bowels move,
>   Thy nature and Thy name is love."

The hymn from which he quoted these glowing lines, and the one beginning, "The God of Abraham praise," he often requested to have read to him. So especially our Lord's words in John xiv. "The great truths of the Gospel," he solemnly observed, "are registered in heaven; my confidence in them is unwavering. I believe that I have preached the truth as it is in Jesus; but, should I be spared to preach again, I would be more simple."

The *South Australian Register* gave the following testimony to his worth:—"Mr. Longbottom was very highly beloved by his own immediate connections, and enjoyed, in a high degree, the respect and esteem of all classes of the colonists, to whom he endeared himself by his amiable and kind deportment, maintaining, to the hour of his death, a consistent uprightness of character, both as a Christian minister and a gentleman." It was not long after that the editor of the *Register* (the able John Stephens) followed him to the grave. The dust of both lies in the West Terrace Cemetery, Adelaide. A tablet to Mr. Longbottom's memory has been erected in the Pirie Street Church. It reads as follows:—

SACRED
TO THE MEMORY OF
THE REV. WILLIAM LONGBOTTOM,
First Wesleyan Missionary to South Australia.
DIED 29TH OF JULY 1849,
IN THE 50TH YEAR OF HIS AGE.

Blessed are the dead which die in the Lord.

This chapter ought not to close without some reference to Mrs. Longbottom. Amongst the pioneer Methodists, and throughout her life in South Australia, she was known as "A Mother in Israel." One of the pioneers says: "The wife of our first pastor was an excellent helpmeet to her husband, very usefully engaged in service for Christ." She visited the sick and poor, and took charge of a class.

Mrs. Longbottom was born in Wakefield, in the year 1796. Her conversion took place under the preaching of the Rev. Joseph Benson. She joined the Methodist Society in 1812, and at once entered upon Christian work. In 1822 she was appointed a leader by the Rev. Richard Watson, and a few years later was married to Mr. Longbottom. She shared the strange vicissitudes that we have described, and survived her husband about twenty-four years.

Mrs. Longbottom had remarkable skill in acquiring languages. In six months after her arrival in India she conducted classes in Tamil and Portuguese. During the short time she spent with her husband at the Cape she acquired such a knowledge of the Dutch language as to be able to pray in public and to lead a class in that tongue. Her long life was devoted to good works. About a week before her death she felt that a change was coming. She asked to be raised in bed, and said : " What is this I feel ? Can it be death ?

> Oh, let me have one smile from Thee
> And drop into eternity."

Turning to her daughter she said : " All is right. I have no fear beyond the grave. Oh no; my trust is in Christ. But I have never yet been delivered from the fear of the article of death."

A friend remarked to her that she was nearly home. "Yes," she replied; "nearly home," and added: "Christ in me, the hope of glory." With peace and calmness she waited for the end. Without one sign of suffering she fell asleep.

REV. DANIEL J. DRAPER

CHAPTER X

AN ABLE ADMINISTRATOR

ABOUT the year 1820 there was a Methodist chapel in the village of Fareham, in Hampshire. Methodist preaching, at this time, was of a very stirring character. Itinerant and local preacher "cried aloud, and spared not." They lifted up their voices "like a trumpet," and showed villagers their transgressions, and citizens their sins.

The trumpet in the village of Fareham gave no uncertain sound. There was a lad living in the adjoining village, named Daniel. Sometimes he would stop at the chapel door to listen. This gave offence. Some of the good people wanted to know why he did not come in or stay away. The reason may have been that his parents were regular attendants at the parish church. On one occasion, as Daniel was gathering up the crumbs that fell from the Master's table, he got a very sharp rebuke. "I will not go there any more," said he. The resolution was made, but it could not be kept. There was a strange magnetism about that Methodist chapel door in the village of Fareham. Daniel felt like Jeremiah when he said: "I will not make mention of Him, nor speak any more in His name; but His word was in my heart as a burning fire shut up in my bones." He was found at the chapel door again, and over the threshold. The word reached his heart. Daniel saw the truth, and grasped it. His parents, as we have affirmed, were members of the Church of England; but it was the stirring blast of the Methodist trumpet that aroused Daniel's conscience and troubled his soul. It was under the Methodist ministry that he found peace. Is it matter for surprise, then, that he should say: "This people shall be my people, and their God shall be my God"? The little Methodist society at Fareham received Daniel into its fold. His parents were not pleased, but we believe that they were too wise to throw any serious obstacle in his way.

In a short time the Methodists decided to build a chapel in the adjoining village of Wickham. It was in this locality that Daniel lived. His father was the chief carpenter and builder in the district, and the work of building was intrusted to him and his son. In this chapel, ere long, the father had the privilege of hearing the son preach the gospel.

When about twenty-two years of age Daniel James Draper removed to Brecon. Here he worked hard in his own mental and spiritual interest, and in the interests of the Methodist society. He gave attention to "reading, exhortation, and doctrine." One of his favourite verses in the prayer-meeting was—

> Happy if with my latest breath
> I may but gasp His name;
> Preach Him to all, and cry in death,
> Behold! Behold! the Lamb.

Little did he anticipate how truly and tragically the desire expressed in this verse would be fulfilled.

While at Brecon he was recommended to the Conference as a suitable candidate for the ministry. The recommendation was sustained, and Daniel James Draper was sent to the Chatteris

Circuit, Cambridgeshire. But there was a wider sphere in which he was to labour. Several Australian Colonies had been formed. The hive in the Old Land was swarming. Thousands were flocking over the sea. "The world is my parish," said John Wesley, and his sons in the gospel had been true to the maxim. Provision had to be made for the spiritual wants of the emigrants. There were men in the Australian Colonies crying to their Methodist fathers and brethren in England: "Come over, and help us." The harvest is great; the labourers few. Strong men are wanted— strong in body, mind, and soul. Such a man was Daniel James Draper. He had a splendid physique; his mental gifts were considerable, and his life consecrated to God. The eyes of some in the British Conference were directed to him. When asked if he would offer for mission work, after a brief consideration he expressed his willingness to obey the call of duty, and to do the will of God. Amongst others who spoke to him words of encouragement, was Dr. Bunting. Said he: "Years of labour may be before you, but success is certain; it must come."

It was about the middle of October 1835 that

a vessel sailed away from Old England, having on board John M'Kenny, Daniel James Draper, and Frederick Lewis. Their destination was New South Wales. John M'Kenny had already spent about twenty years in Foreign Mission work, chiefly in the island of Ceylon. Daniel James Draper and Frederick Lewis were new to the work. The latter part of their voyage was full of peril. The prospect of shipwreck attended the beginning of Daniel James Draper's work, and actual shipwreck brought it to a close.

Says the Rev. John M'Kenny, in a communication to the Missionary Secretaries: " Our passage round was attended with great danger. We experienced a heavy gale from the east. . . . It was indeed an awful night, and brought us all carefully to examine the ground on which we hoped for heaven, having eternity in view. It was now that we felt the infinite value of the gospel, and the exceeding preciousness of Jesus, our glorious Redeemer. Such was the state of things from the violence of the ship's motion, and the sickness of most of the party, that we could not be together; but all were engaged in continued prayer. . . . We did not pray in vain. About one o'clock a.m. our kind captain came round to our cabins and said, in a full voice: 'The wind is changed, and is blowing us off the land, and all danger is over.' Those only who have been in our condition can enter into the exquisite nature of our feelings. An unutterable sensation passed through our minds on finding that the Lord had heard our prayers, and rescued us from destruction and death."

There was a work for John M'Kenny, Daniel James Draper, and Frederick Lewis to do.

Mr. Draper spent about ten years in New South Wales and Victoria. In every station he was successful. Part of his time was spent under a cloud of sorrow, a young wife and child being removed by death.

In the English Minutes of Conference for 1846 the name of Jonathan Innes stands opposite the Adelaide Mission. The appointment did not take effect. In place of Jonathan Innes, Daniel James Draper came. It is to this "man of God" that Methodism in South Australia owes much. The Colony and the Methodist Church were still in their infancy when he arrived—both were but ten years of age. From communications made to the Missionary Secretaries in London we see the spirit in which he entered upon his work. "There is only one Circuit," he says, "in the whole of South Australia." That Circuit was one hundred and fifty miles long, and should be divided into three—Adelaide, Willunga, and North Mines Circuits. Two more missionaries were required. There had been an increase of thirty-three full members on the quarter; the total number was three hundred and fifty. The congregations were exceedingly good. Classes met in private houses. The people, considering their circumstances, were exceedingly liberal. He concludes his letter thus : " If two more ministers can be appointed, we soon shall have a glorious cause in South Australia. Ministerial influence is absolutely necessary."

> Be they many or few, my days are His due,
> And they all are devoted to Him.

Alas! there came another "rift within the lute"; fortunately for Methodism, it did "not make the music mute." In 1846 the Government of South Australia decided to give State aid to religion. Grants-in-aid were to be made available for the Churches. This legislation, as we shall see, had a serious effect upon Methodism. The radical tendencies of Joseph Rayner Stephens and his brother John have already been noticed. They were men with faults, no doubt, but men of bold independent spirit, and as able as bold. Edward Stephens, apparently, was more calm and judicial; still there was the same spirit of independence. The bank manager, no less than the preacher, or editor, was able, energetic, and determined. As soon as the Government decided to give State aid to religion, a number of colonists formed themselves into a League to resist what they considered to be "a dangerous and disgraceful" innovation. At the head of this League was Edward Stephens. In opposition to the grant, public meetings were held; petitions were presented; deputations waited upon the Government. State aid to religion was denounced as a "violation of the rights of conscience." It compelled individuals to pay taxes in support of doctrines and forms over which men differed. It was a misappropriation of public money. In all this justifiable agitation Edward Stephens was the leading spirit.

Mr. Draper, personally, was not opposed to the

grant. Apparently, he remained neutral. The quarterly meeting decided to accept the same, consequently Edward Stephens and several others severed their connection with Wesleyan Methodism.

It is worthy of remark that when a body of men secede from the Methodist Church, as a rule they do not unite with other organisations. Invariably, they endeavour to establish an independent body, and to work it on Methodist lines. What an eloquent testimony this is to the tenacious grip that Methodist doctrine and discipline has upon the hearts of those who come under its influence! As we have observed, ere the Methodist Church in South Australia was seven years old there was a secession. The disaffected party were asked to join other Churches, but asked in vain. The magnetism of Methodism was too strong. They formed themselves into a separate body, termed "The Australian Methodist Society." Fortunately, it had an ephemeral existence. When the division on the question of State aid to religion occurred, the seceders established an independent society. It was called the "Representative Methodist Church." Its life was very limited, as was also the obnoxious law that called the new organisation into existence. Throughout the Colony there was such a cry raised against the grant-in-aid that the Government were forced to repeal the Act. So effectual and determined was the opposition, that the spectre of State aid has never again appeared to disturb the minds of our people. Great credit is due to Edward Stephens for the prominent part that he took in the agitation. No doubt the *Register*, under the able editorship of John Stephens, thundered out its telling anathemas.

In connection with the question of State aid to religion, we find three sons of one of the Presidents of the British Wesleyan Methodist Conference in conflict with their father's Church. It was this subject in the Old Country that led to the retirement of Joseph Rayner Stephens. His brother John, then editor of the *Christian Advocate*, looked upon that retirement as tantamount to expulsion; hence his attacks upon the Methodist Conference —or certain members of it—became increasingly bitter. In the new Colony of South Australia, when the quarterly meeting accepted the Government grant, Edward Stephens retired from the

Connexion. We are all wise after the event. At this length of time it occurs to the writer that there might have been (as Dr. Warren suggested [1]) a "more excellent way" of dealing with Joseph Rayner Stephens, and in this Colony it would have been well if the pioneer Methodist Church had not accepted money from the State coffers.

The withdrawal of Edward Stephens was a heavy blow to the young Methodist Church in South Australia. He was an able and energetic worker, and liberal supporter. Even at this length of time we cannot but regret the circumstance.

But the good work went on. At the close of the year 1847 Mr. Draper posted another letter to the Committee in London. Again there was an increase in members. He speaks of new chapels being opened, and of considerable sums of money being raised. He expresses gratitude that the Circuit had been divided into three Circuits. He says: "I am left alone in Adelaide with sixteen places to attend to, at eight of which we have

---

[1] See Smith's *History of Methodism*, vol. iii. p. 209. There may have been a wiser way of dealing with Joseph Rayner Stephens, but discipline must, at all costs, be maintained.

chapels. I shall have to work excessively hard, until I am assisted by another young man. . . . But such is my conviction of the importance of taking possession of these places, that I am willing to exert myself to the utmost, and to make sacrifices that their case may be met. The Colony requires five ministers at least, in order that our Society may exert its legitimate influence. I rejoice that at so early a period there are three of us here. . . . I cannot, however, be satisfied till we have five in South Australia—Adelaide, two; Willunga, one; North Mines (Burra), one; Mount Barker, one. My heart would rejoice if, on the arrival of the Stations of the Conference of 1848, the above scheme should be fixed, and a reinforcement sent out to enable the district to arrange it. Should I be permitted to witness this, I shall indeed rejoice in the assurance that I have been sent to this Circuit for a most important and valuable end."

Mr. Draper makes a special appeal to the missionary authorities in London, based upon the special relationship that many of the emigrants sustained to the Methodist Church at home. It is an appeal that ought to have touched the hearts of the missionary scribes who dwelt at Bishopsgate Street Within. "Numbers," he says, "of those who are scattered up and down this Colony are from your own congregations in England. Their condition is awful. Our hands are full—improperly so; as to our health, dangerously so. ("I speak as a fool.") We work as hard as any preachers under heaven; but still there are many places that cannot be reached. Do, I beseech you, use every means to supply our wants, and generations yet unborn, in one of the most important of the British Colonies, will bless you. We have now about four hundred and sixty members in Society."

The good man's heart yearns over Zion. The fields are white, but the labourers few. In the interests of "generations unborn" he urges his plea; but apparently "Bishopsgate Street Within" gave no immediate sign. "My heart would rejoice," he says, "if, on the arrival of the Stations of 1848, my scheme should be fixed, and a reinforcement sent out." The good man must have been disappointed. The English Minutes for 1848 do not show that his desire was met. However—

To patient faith the prize is sure.

The English list of stations for 1849 gives the following :—

SOUTH AUSTRALIA.

Adelaide—Daniel J. Draper, Thomas N. Hull, William C. Currey, William Longbottom, supernumerary.

Burra (North Mines)—John C. Thrum.

Willunga—William Lowe.

The Rev. Thomas N. Hull, who arrived from England early in 1850, deserves a passing remark. He was a gifted man. No mean authority (the late Rev. James Bickford) says: "As a preacher he gained celebrity for his logical acumen, refined taste, exalted eloquence, and impressive appeals." After about five years' service he returned to Ireland.

In 1848 Mr. Draper sent statistics of the Methodist Church in the new Colony of South Australia to the missionary authorities in London:—Chapels, 12; other preaching stations, 18; missionaries, 4; Sunday-school teachers, 85; local preachers, 35; class leaders, 30; members, 500; Sunday schools, 12; Sunday-school scholars, 800; attendants upon public worship, 2200.

This is a very creditable record for a Colony only then twelve years old.

The great event of Mr. Draper's administration was the building of the cathedral of South Australian Methodism. The church in Gawler Place, in the erection of which Edward Stephens and his wife had taken such interest, became too small.[1] It was decided to build a large church in a central position. The foundation-stone was laid by the Governor (Sir H. E. Young) on the 15th of July 1850. It was a national event. The entire cost was more than £6000. Without galleries there was sitting accommodation for 800 people.

The church was opened on 19th October 1851. This was another gala day in the early history of the Methodist Church. There was a prayer-meeting at seven o'clock in the morning. The record is: "A good time. Many present." The day was oppressively hot, but the people attended in crowds. Many came in from the country. The Rev. John Eggleston came from New South Wales to conduct

---

[1] The Gawler Place Chapel, in the early days, was a fine structure, but it has long since disappeared. Where it once stood a large business house now stands.

the opening services. Long before the time for beginning the morning service arrived the chapel was crowded. Mr. Draper conducted the first part of the service, and Mr. Eggleston preached the sermon. The text was Ephesians ii. 18. The Rev. J. Gardiner (Presbyterian) preached in the afternoon. The text was Zechariah vi. 13. The chapel was again crowded in the evening, when the Rev. J. Eggleston preached from Isaiah xxvii. 4–6. The Governor, Judge, and several Members of Parliament attended the opening services. The collections were: morning, nearly £68; afternoon, £28, 10s.; evening, £47, 10s. Mr. Draper remarks: "Immense excitement. Good done." On the following Monday there was a tea-meeting on a magnificent scale, realising £46. The opening services were continued on the following Sabbath. The entire amount raised at the services (including a bazaar) was £1250—a noble sum for a Colony and a Church only fifteen years old.

One cannot but regret that in the building of this magnificent chapel Edward Stephens had no prominent part. However, another name was coming to the front—a name that will always be honoured in South Australia, and in South Australian Methodism—John Colton (afterwards Sir John), treasurer of the Pirie Street Chapel Trust. He arrived in the Colony in 1839, and for a great number of years was a leading spirit in Parliament, in philanthropic circles, and in the Wesleyan Methodist Church. His name is on the trust deeds of many of our churches, and it was his hand that laid many of the foundation-stones.

In 1855 Mr. Draper left the Colony. It had not yet reached its majority, but the success and permanence of Methodism was assured. Mr. Draper saw the membership grow from three hundred and fifty members to over a thousand. The finest of any of the churches yet built in the city of Adelaide by any denomination was erected in his time. In addition, a number of chapels had been built in the suburbs and country. He was the principal factor in extending and consolidating the Methodist Church in the new settlement of South Australia.

We close this chapter with an account of the last days of this noted man. We have spoken of " The Romance of Methodism." That there is such, the record we have given amply testifies. But romance has a sad side as well as a joyous one; its dark shades as well as its bright ones. We saw the pioneer Methodist Church in the new Colony in need of a pastor. The need was made the subject of prayer. By the ministry of the winds and the waves an ideal Methodist missionary was cast upon South Australian shores. But in more senses than one, as the sequel will show, the winds and the waves do strange work.

When Mr. Draper left South Australia he returned to Victoria. In 1859 he was elected President of the Australian Conference. After an absence of about thirty years from Old England he felt a strong desire once more to see his native land. The little Methodist chapel in the village of Fareham still attracted him. It would be such a joy to see it once more, and again to tread the lanes that he had so often trodden in his youth. His parents were dead, and many of his early friends were gone, but the village, with the memory of its associations, remained. The buttercups and cowslips would still bloom, the honeysuckle would be as sweet as ever, and there would not be any change in the song of the skylark or the homely note of the cuckoo.

In 1865 Mr. and Mrs. Draper were in the Old Land. He had been appointed Representative to the British Conference. It was held at Birmingham. The fathers and brethren gave him the right hand of fellowship, and he won the esteem of all. He preached in Great Queen Street Chapel, at St. James's Hall, and in the village of Fareham. Here he had the graves of his parents renovated, little thinking how soon he would follow them to the eternal world.

After a short and happy holiday in England he was anxious to return: as he remarked to the Hon. W. M'Arthur, " I could spend another year in England very pleasantly, and should like to do so if my conscience would allow me, but I feel that I must get back to my work."

He engaged a berth for himself and his wife in the S.S. *London*. She sailed from Plymouth on 6th January 1866. There were more than two hundred persons on board:—amongst others: G. V. Brooke, the eminent tragedian, and his sister; also the Rev. Dr. Wooley, an able scholar, who was on his way out to his professorial duties at Sydney. There a wife and six children were waiting to receive him. Alas! they waited in vain.

A day after they sailed the wind increased in violence. There was a very heavy sea. The following day (Monday) some of the passengers became very anxious. The wind was blowing with great violence. Monday night was a night of distress. Many of the passengers read their Bibles together and engaged in prayer. On Tuesday the large vessel was tossed about like a cork, and whole seas dashed over her. The lifeboat was torn away by the winds and the waves. The masts were broken and the ship dismantled. It seemed as though the raging elements were venting their fury upon what was a noble work of man.

Daniel James Draper was not idle. It was not the first storm at sea that he had experienced. About thirty years before, in his first voyage to Australia, in company with John M'Kenny and Frederick Lewis, he had been nearly wrecked. It seemed as though what was once probable would now become actual. No time was to be lost. Now, more truly than ever, he must have felt the inspiration of the words of Christ: " I must work the works of Him who sent Me, while it is day." He began to point the anxious and distressed to the sinner's refuge—Christ.

During the whole of Tuesday night some of the passengers read the Bible in turns.

Early on Wednesday morning the captain tried to run back to Plymouth. The storm increased in fury. The sea ran mountains high. Both lifeboats were swept away. During Wednesday night one disaster after another overtook the ill-fated *London*. The engine-room was flooded with water. The vessel was now so damaged that it seemed impossible to keep out the sea. Various expedients were tried. Passengers and crew worked incessantly at the pumps. Still the water in the engine-room rose higher. The fires were put out. The engines ceased to work. In the midst of all these appalling disasters the noble-hearted Captain Martin remained perfectly calm and collected, never forsaking the post of duty. All that skilful seamanship could do had been done. He now ordered the maintop-sail to be set; but the wind tore it to shreds. "You may now say your prayers, boys," said he.

Thursday morning came. The gale was as fierce as ever. The vessel rolled helplessly in the sea. A tremendous body of water stove in four windows of the upper or poop cabin. The passengers and crew had worked nobly at the pumps, but the vessel was now half-full of water. The remaining boats were got ready. The starboard pinnance was lowered, but was almost immediately swamped and sunk. Captain Martin went down into the saloon. "Ladies," said he, "there is no hope for us, I am afraid; nothing short of a miracle can save us." Said Mr. Draper, very calmly, "Let us pray." The vessel was now settling down.

Mr. Draper was constant in his ministrations. Ah! there were grief-stricken fathers and mothers and little children to be comforted and encouraged. The only comfort now was the hope of meeting in heaven. The passengers were urged to "flee for refuge to the hope set before them." "Pray for me, Mr. Draper; pray for me," was the cry. What cries went up to heaven from that doomed vessel! Mr. Draper pleading for the salvation of souls, and passengers seeking pardon! "Prepare to meet thy God!" was the cry of the Methodist preacher. "My friends," said he, "our captain tells us there is no hope, but the great Captain above tells us there is hope, and that we may all get safe to heaven." Prayer was heard and answered. Before the vessel went down there was wonderful calmness on board—a spirit of patient resignation. Husbands, wives, and children clung to each other, going simultaneously—not down into the deep, but into the eternal joy and peace of heaven.

A boat was launched. Ah! there were deeds of heroism on board the sinking vessel. A husband was offered by a friend a place in the boat. "No," said he; "I promised my wife and children to stay with them, and I will do so." . . . "Help me," he said, "to move the children to the other side, out of the water." He did so. They then parted—the friend to escape in the boat to tell the tale; the husband, wife, and children to pass into the eternal world. "They were lovely and pleasant in their lives, and in death they were not divided." The men in the boat wished Captain Martin to join them. "No," said he; "I will go down with the passengers. Your course is E.N.E." Then, throwing them a compass, he added: "I wish you God-speed, and safe to land." Soon after, the vessel went down stern foremost. Nineteen persons escaped in the boat, and were ultimately picked up by an Italian barque. "When I left the ship," said one of the survivors, "the passengers had given up all hope, but there was a remarkable composure among them, and no loud sounds to be heard. I heard voices engaged in preaching and praying." The last words that the survivors heard Daniel James Draper say were: "Those of you who are not converted, now is the time; not a moment to be lost, for in a few minutes we shall all be in the presence of our Judge." It is said that he was calm and self-possessed, his wife standing by his side.

When a local preacher in Brecon he had often sung—

> Happy if with my latest breath
> I may but gasp His name;
> Preach Him to all, and cry in death,
> Behold! Behold! the Lamb.

How tragically the sentiment of the verse was realised!

From that dark and dreadful scene in the Bay of Biscay there come to us rays of light. Said the heroic Methodist preacher: "Those of you who are not converted, now is the time." ... "There is hope that we may all get safe to heaven." It is probable that that hope was fulfilled. Said the dying thief at the last hour: "Lord, remember me when Thou comest in Thy kingdom." The cheering response was: "To-day shalt thou be with Me in paradise." To the penitent, perishing, praying men and women on board the doomed *London*, would there not come the same blessed assurance? Hence the absence of panic—the "peace that passeth all understanding," the trustful resignation. As a person was about to leap into the boat, a young girl put a piece of paper into his hand. On it was written: "Dear mother, you must not grieve for me. I am going to Jesus."

If we keep our eyes fixed on the dark aspect of the wreck that we have depicted, our hearts will be inexpressibly sad. To see fathers, mothers, and children locked in each other's embrace, and going down into the angry deep, with a love that was quenchless, is almost too much for human reason.

Alas! we are the slaves of our senses. The most real and abiding things on earth are the things that are invisible. The most real thing about the person who is writing this sketch is not the visible and tangible hand that holds the pen, but the invisible and intangible agent that conceives the thoughts, translates them into words, marshals the sentences, and compels the hand to do its bidding—the mysterious "I" that knows itself as distinct from the body. Don't look merely at the lost bodies on the ill-fated *London*, but at the saved souls. "And the Lord opened the eyes of the young man; and he saw: and, behold, the mountain was full of horses and chariots of fire round about Elisha" (2 Kings vi. 17). "And Lazarus died, and was carried by the angels into Abraham's bosom." Not the corruptible body, but the living, energising, intelligent soul, by the eye of faith, in the light of Divine revelation, crosses the boundary line of sensual experience. See the spirits of the shipwrecked passengers escorted to paradise—fathers, mothers, and children entering simultaneously into one of the palaces of the great King. Yes. "In My Father's house are many mansions: if it were not so, I would have told you. I go to prepare a place for you. And if I go and prepare a place for you, I will come again, and receive you unto Myself; that where I am, there ye may be also." Grasp this comforting assurance, and our wail of sorrow becomes a shout of victory.

As South Australian Methodists, we thank God for the work of consolidation and extension that Daniel James Draper did in the young Colony, and for his comforting, encouraging, and soul-saving ministry on board the doomed *London*. A fine church in Adelaide has been erected to his memory.

ADELAIDE IN 1896: KING WILLIAM STREET

CHAPTER XI

AFTER SIXTY YEARS

MORE than sixty years ago South Australia was a *terra incognita*. Its interior was as little known as the back side of the moon. No white foot had trodden its vast plains nor climbed its lofty hills. It was like a well-appointed domicile, awaiting a suitable tenant. It was made to be inhabited by the highest type of man, and until the purpose of its creation was realised there was something awanting and amiss. There was no lowing of oxen, nor bleating of sheep; no ploughman's whistle, nor milkmaid's song; no long, freshly-turned furrows, nor fields of waving corn. The air had not vibrated with the sound of horse's hoof nor the rumble of wheels. The music of the whetted scythe no ear had heard. There were no roads, bridges, fences, nor houses surrounded with flowers and fruit-bearing trees. Save the loud laugh of the jackass, the howl of the dingo, or the war-whoop of the blackfellow, few startling noises were heard.

The country abounded in game. Kangaroos and wallabies roamed about in flocks. Here and there families of wombats dwelt in their holes. The emu and her chicks sped over the plain. On the lakes were wild fowl, and the Murray teemed with fish. Where Adelaide now stands serpents glided and kangaroos fed.

The blackfellow held undisputed sway. His was a free-and-easy kind of life. Except the fear of sorcery, and an occasional tribal fight, there was little to trouble his soul. The day was spent in eating and drinking, making weapons or canoes, netting wild fowl, hunting the kangaroo, and spearing fish. At night there was the mystic corrobery. It consisted of a wild, weird song and dance. Sometimes the dance was very lewd. As a rule, the men danced. The women sat on the ground, and kept time by the knocking of waddies together, or striking rolls of skins with the fist.

Infanticide was a common practice. Often a child was killed as soon as it was born.

But there were good as well as evil traits. We have spoken of a few wild white men (whalers and sealers) who had found their way to the South Australian coast before colonisation took place. The Rev. George Taplin, who spent many years among the natives, tells a story that he had heard of those early days. "Some white sealers, on Kangaroo Island, stole from the mainland, near Cape Jervis, three native women, and took them to the island. When the prisoners had stayed with their captors a few weeks, they began to cast about for means to get back to their husbands and friends. At last they found a small dingy belonging to the sealers. It would only hold two. Two of the women had no children, but the third had an infant at the breast; so the two childless lubras took the dingy and started for the mainland, reaching it in safety. The poor mother, left behind with her babe, must have pined sadly for her country and friends; but nothing was heard of her for some time. One day the natives found her body on the beach, just above high-water mark, with her baby tied on her back. She had swum Backstairs Passage (about nine miles in the narrowest part, and infested with sharks), and then, in a state of utter exhaustion, crawled up the shore, and died."

We have seen the first colonist (Samuel Stephens) put his foot on Australian shore. We have seen the early emigrants' tents pitched amongst the trees and rushes that skirted the shores of Holdfast Bay. Beds made of rushes; pork barrels and packing cases extemporised as tables; emigrants dragging their goods to the site of a city that was yet to be, have passed before our view. Where those tents, sixty-two years ago, were pitched, the large and aristocratic town of Glenelg now stands, which has some of the finest streets that the Southern Hemisphere can show, and its system of deep drainage is unsurpassed. Trams are running in all directions. Through country that sixty years ago was unexplored and unknown, trains now rush, laden with passengers, wheat, wool, sheep, cattle, and mineral wealth. There is a beautiful park round the city; outside are crowded suburbs. The population in and around Adelaide alone has been estimated at about one hundred thousand. Dotted over the country are towns, villages, gardens, and farms. It seems like a fairy tale. All has been accomplished in less than threescore years and ten. Sixty-two years ago the population was about five hundred; to-day it is more than three hundred and twenty thousand.

In 1886 we celebrated our Jubilee. Speaking on that occasion, Sir Henry Ayers, one of the early emigrants, said: " Something must be said of the country we have been in the possession of for fifty years. It may not unreasonably be demanded of us to state what use we have made of the talents committed to our care for the benefit of mankind. We have utilised, for pastoral purposes, many thousand square miles of country, on which depasture some seven millions of sheep, three million head of cattle, and over one hundred and seventy thousand horses. We have brought under cultivation nearly three millions of acres. We have made it a country productive of wool, of corn, of fruit, of wine, of oil, and a land flowing with milk and honey. We have completed telegraphic communication across the continent, and thus brought Australia within speaking distance of all parts of the world. We have constructed over a thousand miles of railway and many thousands of miles of macadamised road. We have erected various buildings, and built bridges, docks, wharves, jetties, and other works required for our wants. We have made ample provision for educating the people, including the establishment and endowment of a university. We have founded hospitals and asylums for the insane, the sick, the incurable, the blind, the dumb, the deaf, the orphan, and the necessitous poor. . . . But some captious critic may say, All these things are for yourselves; tell us what you have done for your brethren abroad? We have fed the people of the outside world with breadstuffs to the value of some thirty-five millions sterling. We have clothed them with some forty millions' worth of wool. . . . We have sent them nearly twenty millions sterling of minerals and metals. Could the greatest optimist among the early settlers have predicted such results?"

The natives have not been forgotten. During the last sixty years several mission stations have been established. The most successful has been the mission at Point M'Leay. For many years it was under the able superintendence of the Rev. George Taplin, who deserves a niche in South Australian history. Missionary efforts among the Aborigines in this Colony have been very much neutralised by the conduct of lecherous whites.

We saw the early emigrants at Holdfast Bay leaving their bough-booths and canvas tents, and wending their way to the tent of Edward Stephens, in which John White preached the first Methodist sermon on the mainland. Later on (when the site for Adelaide had been fixed) we saw a few Methodists assembled in a hut, on the banks of the Torrens, to consider the advisability of forming a Methodist Society. The number of names was fifteen. They had neither church nor travelling preacher. What do we see to-day, after the lapse of sixty years? In addition to many preaching places, there are—

Churches	271
Ministers	66
Local preachers	422
Sunday-school workers	2,596

Sunday-school scholars	22,886
Church members	8,527
Adherents	49,204

Our returns would be larger, but several of our members and ministers, of late years, have removed to Western Australia. There are results that we cannot tabulate, such as the number of souls who, during the sixty years of our history, have gone from the Methodist Church militant to join the Church triumphant.

We have only given the statistics for the Wesleyan Methodist Church. Two other vigorous Methodist Societies have been established—the *Primitive Methodist* and the *Bible Christian.*

The first Primitive Methodist service in the new Colony was held in the open air. This was one Sunday afternoon, in June 1840. The place of meeting was Light Square, Adelaide, and the service was conducted by a few laymen. A few years later the pioneer preachers arrived. The Revs. J. Long and J. Wilson came out in 1844, and the Rev. W. Storr in 1846. These have all "entered into rest." To-day the Primitive Methodist body number—

Churches	118
Ministers	29
Local preachers	220
Sunday-school workers	886
Sunday-school scholars	7,021
Members	3,181
Adherents	14,291

The pioneer preachers of the Bible Christian body arrived in 1850. They were the Revs. James Way and James Rowe. The former has passed away. He was the father of the Right Hon. S. J. Way, Chief Justice and Lieutenant-Governor of South Australia. The venerable James Rowe is still with us. These brethren established the Bible Christian Society. To-day that Society numbers—

Churches	131
Ministers	38
Local preachers	253
Sunday-school workers	980
Sunday-school scholars	8,176
Members	4,007
Adherents (about)	16,000

This makes a grand total of Methodist progress, *in South Australia alone*, for sixty years as follows:—

Churches	520
Ministers	133

Local preachers	895
Sunday-school workers	4,462
Sunday-school scholars	38,083
Members	15,715
Adherents	79,495

Yet some say that Methodism is dying, or is in a very decrepit state. Surely such critics must move in a very circumscribed sphere, or be subject to some strange hallucination. Still we need to keep our armour bright, tenaciously to grasp the shield of faith, and vigorously to wield the sword of the Spirit. The age in which we live is peculiar. The struggle for existence is keen. The love for amusement has become irrational. The " Higher Criticism " has not been spiritually helpful. It is a difficult matter to make men see and feel the exceeding sinfulness of sin. Religious indifference is widespread. Men say : " Where is the promise of His coming ? for since the fathers fell asleep all things continue as they were from the beginning of the creation." " This worldliness " has become predominant. A social gospel is being preached that is merely the skeleton of the Christian religion. The " man of sin " is at work amongst the masses. There is a growing tendency to subvert social order, and to set at nought authority. If we have our fathers' zeal we have not our fathers' success. The vitality, permanence, and extension of Methodism depends upon soul-converting energy.

Sixty-three years ago one of the great men of middle Methodism (Peter M'Owan) said: "While other Churches regard revivals as gracious singularities in their history, we ought to consider their frequent occurrence as essential to our very existence. Few persons join our communion till they are awakened from the sleep of nature; for our doctrines, as a whole, are such that natural men cannot receive; our discipline is such that they cannot, for any length of time, brook; and as the chief term on which we admit to membership is a 'desire to flee from the wrath to come,' it is not to be expected that they will seek admission till they feel themselves really exposed to wrath. If conversion work, therefore, were to cease among us, the extinction of our societies, or a radical change in the spiritual character of our economy, would be inevitable." These are wise words—true as they are wise; and we ought seriously to ponder them.

If the soul-converting power ceases—if *intellectualism* takes the place of *evangelicism*—Methodism must decline, and cease to be.

Let us lay other wise words of the same Methodist preacher to heart. He says: "We stand in the relation of fathers to the generations yet to come, and it is our indispensable duty to pray that the system which has proved in the hands of the Spirit of God saving to ourselves may not be deteriorated by our means. . . . We found it distinguished by an evangelical creed, a heart-searching and awakening ministry, and we must pray that the spirit-stirring energy of our pulpit ministrations may be preserved and increased. . . . We found it spiritual in its economy and leading design, and on no account must we prostitute it to the purposes of party politics. We found its genius aggressive and inspiring, so far as the destruction of the kingdom of darkness is concerned; and if we would benefit mankind, we must foster this thirst for conquest. . . . We found it, in an especial sense, benignant to the poor, and divinely fitted to benefit the outcast portion of our population; and if we would escape the curse of those who rob the poor, we must not mar its happy adaptation to enrich and save the thousands who still have occasion to cry, 'No man careth for my soul.' . . . Though I am neither a prophet nor the son of a prophet, yet I venture to predict that if we thus go on, enlarging and maturing the work at home,—if we fearlessly preach the doctrines of the Cross, and humbly depend upon the energy of the Holy Spirit; if we continue to send out converted missionaries to the heathen; if we persevere in fostering feelings of loyalty to our sovereign, of charity to our brethren of other denominations, and of love to each other; and if all this be done in the spirit of prayer, and with a single eye to the Divine glory, we shall then succeed in consummating the lofty and benevolent enterprise which our fathers commenced; we shall prove that Methodism is but in its infancy, not only in respect of age, but of efficiency; we shall accelerate the final victory, which is to place the sceptres of the earth in the hand and the crowns of the earth on the head of Immanuel."

PRINTED BY MORRISON AND GIBB LIMITED, EDINBURGH

BOOKS OF
TRAVEL, ADVENTURE, and HISTORY.

BY CANOE AND DOG TRAIN AMONG THE CREE AND SALTEAUX INDIANS.
By EGERTON R. YOUNG. Introduction by Rev. MARK GUY PEARSE. Twentieth Thousand. With Photographic Portraits of the Rev. E. R. YOUNG and Mrs. YOUNG. Map, and Thirty-two Illustrations. 3s. 6d.

"One of the most thrilling narratives of missionary life and adventure ever published."—*Birmingham Daily Gazette.*

STORIES FROM INDIAN WIGWAMS AND NORTHERN CAMP-FIRES.
By Rev. EGERTON R. YOUNG, Author of "By Canoe and Dog Train." Ninth Thousand. Forty-three Illustrations. Imperial 16mo, 3s. 6d.

"I regard it as one of the most fascinating, instructive, and stimulating of modern missionary books."—Dr. ARTHUR T. PIERSON.

THREE BOYS IN THE WILD NORTH LAND.
By EGERTON R. YOUNG, Author of "By Canoe and Dog Train among the Cree and Salteaux Indians," "Oowikapun," etc. Twenty-eight full-page Illustrations. Crown 8vo, gilt edges, 3s. 6d.

OOWIKAPUN;
Or, How the Gospel reached the Nelson River Indians. By EGERTON R. YOUNG, Author of "By Canoe and Dog Train," "Stories from Indian Wigwams and Northern Camp-Fires." Fourth Thousand. Illustrated. Imperial 16mo, 2s. 6d.

"Another stirring and delightful volume by the Rev. E. R. Young. It has all the delightful and entertaining features of the best fiction."—*Lincolnshire Free Press.*

ACROSS SIBERIA ON THE GREAT POST ROAD.
By CHARLES WENYON, M.D. With Portrait, Map, and Twenty-seven Illustrations. Third Thousand. Imperial 16mo, 3s. 6d.

"One of the pleasantest books of travel we have read for some time. One lays it down with the feeling of parting from a congenial fellow-traveller on a long and memorable journey."—*Sheffield Independent.*

TWO MEN OF DEVON IN CEYLON.
A Story of East and West. By S. LANGDON, Author of "My Mission Garden," etc. Ten Illustrations. Imperial 16mo, 3s. 6d.

"An unusually fine historical romance."—*Christian Endeavour.*

"The story is told in a fine swelling Lorna-Doone manner."—*The Scotsman.*

"Pleasantly-written and healthy volume, the very thing for our young folk."—*Christian Miscellany.*

"The book is full of incident, and gives much information as to the history and religion of Ceylon."—*Canadian Methodist Magazine.*

CHARLES H. KELLY,
2, CASTLE STREET, CITY ROAD, E.C.; AND 26, PATERNOSTER ROW, E.C.

BOOKS OF TRAVEL, ADVENTURE, and HISTORY—continued.

FOUR YEARS IN UPPER BURMA.

By Rev. W. R. WINSTON. Profusely Illustrated, and a Map. Imperial 16mo, 3s. 6d.

"The volume is abundantly illustrated, and Mr. Winston is so agreeable a writer, and has so much of interest to relate, that his contribution to our knowledge of Burma is most profitable, and calls for warm approval."—*Birmingham Gazette.*

"The country and its pleasant people are described very fully. The historical matter is ably summarised and followed by an account of missionary work. The photographic groups help to a close familiarity." *Leeds Mercury.*

WYCLIFFE TO WESLEY.

Heroes and Martyrs of the Church in Britain. Third Thousand. With Twenty-four Portraits and Forty other Illustrations. Imperial 16mo, 3s. 6d.

"We give a hearty welcome to this handsomely-got-up and interesting volume."—*Literary World.*

RAMBLES IN BIBLE LANDS.

By the Rev. RICHARD NEWTON, D.D. Seventy Illustrations. Imperial 16mo, 3s. 6d.

"An admirable book." *Methodist Recorder.*

"From the juvenile standpoint we can speak in hearty commendation of it."—*Literary World.*

OUR INDIAN EMPIRE: ITS RISE AND GROWTH.

By the Rev. J. S. BANKS, Author of "Martin Luther, the Prophet of Germany," etc. etc. Thirty-five Illustrations, and a Map. Imperial 16mo, 3s. 6d.

"The imagination of the young will be fired by its stirring stories of English victories, and it will do much to make history popular."—*Daily Chronicle.*

"A well-condensed and sensibly-written popular narrative of Anglo-Indian history."—*Daily News.*

POPERY AND PATRONAGE;

Or, Biographical Illustrations of Scotch Church History. By Rev. J. MARRAT. Eleven Illustrations. Imperial 16mo, 3s. 6d.

"The purpose of the writer has been to give concise sketches of Scotch Church history. This he has done in an interesting and almost romance-like fashion, weaving episodes of history around some great central historic figure."—*Liverpool Daily Post.*

OUR SEA-GIRT ISLE.

English Scenes and Scenery Delineated. By Rev. J. MARRAT. 217 Illustrations, and Map. Revised and Enlarged Edition. Imperial 16mo, 3s. 6d.

"A very pleasant companion."—*Daily Telegraph.*

"Bright and pleasant, full of information and good feeling."—*Literary World.*

"An unusually readable and attractive book."—*Christian Age.*

CHARLES H. KELLY,
2, CASTLE STREET, CITY ROAD, E.C.; AND 26, PATERNOSTER ROW, E.C.

www.ingramcontent.com/pod-product-compliance
Lightning Source LLC
Chambersburg PA
CBHW021840230426
43669CB00008B/1032